BACTERIOLOGICAL WARFARE

A MAJOR THREAT TO NORTH AMERICA

WHAT YOU AND YOUR FAMILY CAN DO
BEFORE - AND - AFTER

LARRY WAYNE HARRIS
REGISTERED MICROBIOLOGIST

WARNING

Self-medication under circumstances <u>where a physician's care is available</u> is not only unlawful, it is <u>extremely dangerous.</u> The author and the publisher of this book do not recommend or endorse self-medication or the practice of medicine without a license in any way, shape, or form. The responsibility for any such activity is borne entirely by the reader. **Seek professional medical help if there is any way to obtain it.**

About the Author

I was born in the hills of southwestern Virginia and raised by my fraternal grandparents Curvin and Alpha Harris. I lost my parents when I was less than two years old.

During my childhood my grandparents told me many stories about the great Swine Flu epidemic of 1918. Grandpa Curvin was in the U.S. Army and was stationed in Vancouver, Washington during 1917-1918 when the swine flu first appeared. The initial symptoms were very mild. You felt ill but no one was sick enough to miss work. Some army bases in Texas were also reporting personnel with similar symptoms. Many of these troops were bound for the trenches of WWI then raging in Europe. During many of these battles, mustard gas (a known mutagen) was being used. Shortly after this, a killer flu developed that was known as the Spanish Madden. Troops returning to the United States brought this killer flu with them and spread it throughout the country. Grandma Alpha was living near her parents in the coal mining community of Bradshaw in eastern Kentucky. Curvin had just returned from the Army and he and Alpha had just started keeping house when the killer flu hit. Since Curvin had already contracted and had recovered from the swine flu in its earlier mild form, he was immune. Likewise, his brothers George and Bill were among the very few who were immune and did not catch the flu in its now killer form. In a few days just about everyone was literally down with the flu. In a few more days large numbers of people were dying.

Scenes out of the middle ages, when plague ravaged Europe, appeared. Curvin and his brothers started digging graves as fast as they could, but soon individual graves could not be dug fast enough. Soon, parts of families, sometimes entire families had to be buried in common graves. In a few days, with their strength almost gone, they had to start storing bodies in a coal mine, stacking them up like cord wood.

A single road ran through the town with row houses on either side. The north side was called Noah's Ark, and the south side was called the Titanic. At one end of the town was a large diner that served the miners. Curvin and his brothers placed large wash tubs on the two large cook stoves in the diner. They put in vegetables and beef and began to make beef stew which they then distributed around the community as few were able to cook. After distributing food they would return to the diner and hitch up the horses to a large freight wagon and go house to house collecting the dead, afterwards placing them in the mine.

Over 20 million people worldwide died from the flu. The Bradshaw community was hard hit. Curvin and Alpha had lost their first child, a little girl.

As a result of the many stories about the swine flu epidemic of 1918 I vowed to become a microbiologist when I grew up that I may be able to prevent another plague like that from ever happening again.

My first microscope (used) and lab equipment were purchased with money I received from muskrat pelts that I trapped. I converted an out building into my "mad scientist" laboratory and pursued my passion of microbiology. It was fortunate that I had my own laboratory as I was denied access to the high schools lab after I accidentally blew it up in 1968. In 1988, while visiting my old home town, I saw the teacher who was in the lab the day it exploded. He informed me he still had not gotten all of the glass out.

During my senior year in high school (1969), I told the Army Recruiter I would enlist upon graduation on the condition he could find me a place where I could work in a microbiology laboratory. A few days later I got a letter informing me that he had located a laboratory at the Aberdeen Proving Grounds in Maryland where I could be stationed. Upon graduation I enlisted in the army and after basic training I was stationed at Aberdeen Proving Grounds. Subsequent to the military I have continued my expertise employed by private industry.

I am certified by the American Academy of Microbiology and listed in the *National Registry of Microbiologist*. I am also a **Registered Microbiologist** in clinical and public health, State Board Of Sanitarian Registration, Sanitarian-in-Training. I am a member of The American Society For Microbiology as well.

Preface

In September 1991 I re-entered the Ohio State University and started taking courses in advanced microbiology in preparation for taking my National Registry of Microbiologist Certification Exam. I soon joined a clique of nontraditional students whose average age was around 40. In that clique was Mariam Arif, a delightful lady that soon became a close friend.

Mariam was from Iraq and was here studying microbiology. She had an unusual background. One of her very close relatives, General Arif, had been a President of Iraq. In April 1966 he was killed in a helicopter accident. A long succession of military coups ended in Saddam Hussein and the Republican guard coming to power. During the coups Mariam's family had suffered much. She said that several members of her family had been hung. She felt it safer to be in America until she could do something that would make her famous back in her home country of Iraq.

One morning in February 1993 I had arrived early to get a parking spot in the rapidly filling student parking lots and was having coffee in the small vending area of the Med-Tech building where our courses were taught. The vending area was deserted except for Mariam Arif and myself. I will never forget the way her face and eyes looked that morning -- very tired and glossy. I have no doubt that she had gotten little sleep since the World Trade Center bombing. This was the Monday after.

She must have thought that her arrest was imminent. She was rambling on as if she were in a daze. She was silent for a few minutes then she said, "Larry you are a dear and trusted friend and what I am going to tell you in the next few minutes you can use to protect yourself and a few friends. When it is my time to act, I do not want your death to be on my conscience. You obviously do not know the danger you face concerning the emergence of Biological Warfare as a major threat to the United States." She went on to state that nearly all the emerging countries: Libya, Iran, Iraq, Syria, North Korea, etc., were actively pursuing a Germ Warfare program and scrapping their nuclear program. There are two primary reasons for this shift. The first is the acquisition cost of a sufficiently large nuclear stockpile to be effective. The second reason is BW is antipersonnel warfare, not antimaterial warfare. Housing, buildings, factories, and machinery remain intact and can be made useful in a short time.

I asked her if she had seen any of Iraq's germ warfare facilities. She gave a resounding "Yes!" She stated that Iraq uses the *plain Jane approach* in that Iraq has a very large stockpile of biological agents on hand in the form of special bombs. They are also developing rockets to spread the infection over a very large area. Iraq has two separate areas of biological operations, one foreign and one regional. The ones that are regional have all the facilities located at small airstrips around the country. They are deliberately designed not to draw much attention. These airstrips will not handle large or even medium class aircraft. They only handle a single class of aircraft -- single engine, high wing, turbo props that can be used for crop dusting. The regional biological operations would take only a couple of days if you are using Anthrax, or a couple of weeks if you are using Plague to get in operation. If they were ever questioned from abroad as to the purpose of the chemostats located at these facilities they can be explained away as holding tanks for agriculture spray products if they are kept empty.

To get them into operation they are first cycled through a sterilization phase. Then a special nutrient broth is introduced and the desired biological agent (usually Anthrax or Plague) is added. Devices for rapidly mixing the culture vessel are started and ultra filtered air is bubbled through the nutrient. Fresh nutrient broth (growth medium) from a reservoir is fed at a constant rate to the culture vessel through a metering pump. A constant volume of culture is maintained by means of an overflow that removes culture fluid and the desired bacteria at the same rate as fresh medium is added. The culture fluid flows into a refrigerated tank for holding. It is transferred to the aircraft just before the mission. She further stated that these aircraft have exceptionally long range and that only one aircraft is located at each facility. If that aircraft were lost, a replacement aircraft would be flown in from another facility. This kept every thing small and very difficult to detect. I asked her why we didn't see any Germ Warfare being waged during the Gulf War. To this she responded "We did! The Iraqi military adhered, at least in part, to Soviet military doctrine. Soviet methodology is that chemical warfare should be conducted with mixed agents. Mixed agents, often referred to as 'cocktails,' are intended to enhance the capabilities of nerve agents and defeat the precautions taken by the enemy. Cocktails can be made by combining a wide variety of biological toxins, nerve agents, vesicants, and some biological agents -- such as bacteria and fungi.

Mariam stated that she had personally worked in a germ warfare laboratory in which they had taken Mycoplasma fermentans (incognitus) and had inserted most of the envelope gene from HIV. This genetic manipulation rendered a relative benign mycoplasma much more invasive and pathogenic and capable of attacking many organs and tissue systems in the body. (This can be treated effectively with tetracycline as mentioned later in this book) Mariam also stated that they also had isolated and used a form of Ebola Zaire virus that took over 3 to 7 years to kill you. Within the next few years hundreds of thousands of Desert Storm veterans along with their families will start dying. She said "Iraq thought that the multinational force would respond with Nuclear Weapons if they had used fast acting biologicals."

"You stated that the people of North America are in grave danger of biological agents being used against us. Would you care to elaborate on that?" To this she replied, "A few hours ago a band of fanatics blew up the World Trade Center. I am sure that my beloved Iraq did not do this thing. <u>For when payback comes, I am sure we will demand at least one American life for every one of my countrymen that you butchered. We would not settle for some silly old building.</u>" I asked her if she knew how such an attack would be carried out. To this she responded, "Don't be silly. Of course, I know! All operations will be batch operations. Unlike the very complex chemostat, where you have a continuous output once you are up and running, with a batch all you require is a sterile vessel. This can be a test tube or a larger container depending on your batch size. In this vessel you place the appropriate amount of dehydrated media. This is very easily obtainable in this country without any questions. Then you add the proper amount of distilled water, bring to a boil, and simmer at least 15 minutes. Then let it cool to room temperature. This way you do not have to have an autoclave. The top of the container is covered with sterile cloth that you sterilized inside of a pressure cooker much like the one you cook in. The batch vessel of choice would be a <u>metal</u> spray can (stainless steel) much like the one used to spray your garden or one exterminators use to dispense bug spray. The preferable model is the one that has the little air pump in the middle which you pump up when you are ready to spray. To this you would add your culture. A small heating pad is placed around the tank. Next, a small air stone and tubing (similar to the one used in an aquarium) are boiled for at least an hour and then very aseptically placed in the metal spray can and hooked up to an aquarium air pump. Introduce your plague or anthrax starter culture and after an appropriate amount of time the batch is ready. You then insert the spray tank's air pump, pump up the sprayer, and you are ready."

I then asked her what the most likely targets would be. She replied, "For one thing it will not be a target but rather many (hundreds of) targets simultaneously across the country. A prime one of these would be the subway systems. Who would notice another maintenance man down there spraying for bugs? Other inviting targets are the air ducts of large office buildings. Or, say, a large gathering of people at a stadium, or simpler yet just sticking it outside of a building over those crowded streets in many cities. Who is going to notice a little mist coming from some building? Several cells (each cell has ten men and one woman to act as a carrier) will be using aircraft venturies like the ones that are used to drive the vacuum instruments on airplanes. They are easily obtained mail order or from an aircraft supply in this country. These will be mounted underneath vehicles. The spray tank will be inside with tubing going to the venturi (which acts like a carburetor). When the vehicle is going 60 miles per hour one simply opens the valve and a fog of death will be coming out behind the car. Other cells will be using these same venturies mounted on light aircraft to attack whole cities at a time."

I asked her how she would get her bacteria culture. Mariam replied that it is easy for a woman to hide a small sealed vial of dehydrated culture inside her body cavity. She said "What are they going to do? Take every woman entering the country to a little room in the airport, make them lay on a table with their feet up in straps and have some one look up their private of privates? I think not!"

I then asked her "Why not use something that you could obtain in this country without going to the effort of smuggling?" To this she replied "Iraq purchased all of the dehydrated cultures from companies right here in the United States. They shipped them to Iraq and those same vials are the ones Iraqi women have been bringing back to use against this country. Ironic, isn't it?" Mariam said she had made several trips back and forth between Iraq and the United States, and every time she came to America she was carrying a vial secreted in her body cavity.

"What are the microbes of choice?" I asked her. She responded "Plague and anthrax are the bacteria of choice. You see, plague is easy to work with. We take the proper amount and kind of antibiotic and we are reasonably safe. When you are finished you can easily clean up any spills with disinfectant, and any you miss will be dead in a couple of days regardless. Anthrax, on the other hand, will be used by specially trained groups for attacks on big cities. These cells (groups) have to be extremely careful, thus the detailed training. If you got some on your clothes and happened to inhale it several years later, it could kill you. So they will strip and thoroughly shower. All articles of clothing worn during the attack and preparation will be left behind." She further commented "Cholera and typhoid fever were also considered, but these usually do not kill and only inconvenience people for a few days."

When asked when she thought these attacks would begin she responded "Some time in the next few years. The attacks are centered on three Muslim holy days that occur in the next few years. The first one comes up in July 1997, the next in 1999, the next 2001. One thing is certain, before the year 2002 the population of the United States will be reduced to less than 50 million." Mariam seemed a lot calmer now and her composure was returning. She said, "Larry why don't you meet me on the third story of the main library this afternoon? We can go up into the towers and find a place where we can have some privacy. I need to slip back to my apartment and get some things I want to show you."

That afternoon I met Mariam in the main library where we found a secluded place up in the towers. Mariam opened her briefcase and took out a map of the United States. On the map were little blue squares. Beside each square were a number, and latitude and longitude designations. It was a map of this nation's power grid.

She indicated that in this country electric power is generated at 12,000 volts and then stepped up to over one hundred thousand volts for transmission. These step-up transformers are unique, they are custom built for each power plant. They are oil filled and have large cooling radiators on the sides. To her knowledge there are no backups because they are so expensive.

These transformers are this nation's Achilles heel. They are out in the open, and easy to get at with a special little goody that Iraq has designed. The little blue squares are those step-up transformers and the numbers are cell members whose final job, before they head back to the middle east, is to take out these step-up transformers. The latitude and longitude are for these transformers and are so precise that if it becomes necessary they could lay in a 81mm mortar.

Mariam took out of her briefcase a set of blue prints and said "This is the little goody that Iraq has come up with to take out the transformers. You simply go to the hardware store right here in America and buy a 9 inch piece of 5/8 inch all thread and a 3 inch piece. You then either buy a small 4 inch lathe or, better yet, go to any of a number of small machine shops who will not ask many questions and simply have them follow the design. You will end up with the following:

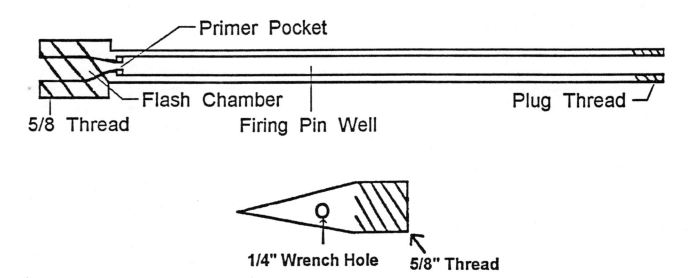

Next, take a 6 inch long piece of 1/4 inch bar stock and fabricate the inertial firing pin

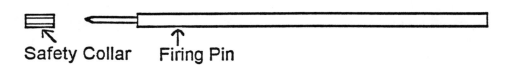

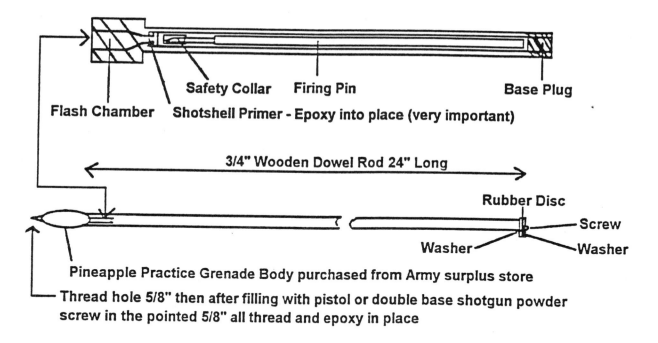

Safety Collar   **Firing Pin**

Base Plug

Flash Chamber   **Shotshell Primer - Epoxy into place (very important)**

3/4" Wooden Dowel Rod 24" Long

Rubber Disc

Screw

Washer   **Washer**

Pineapple Practice Grenade Body purchased from Army surplus store

Thread hole 5/8" then after filling with pistol or double base shotgun powder screw in the pointed 5/8" all thread and epoxy in place

Mariam said "Then purchase a 4 foot long segment of heavy walled water pipe. Slide the rifle grenade in one end of the pipe, pour in a very accurately measured black powder charge, and put in a wooden dowel rod fitted with two tight fitting rubber o-rings, and an electrical igniter. Very dry sea sand, acquired at the same aquarium shop where we got the air stones, is poured in until it completely fills the back end, then the back end is sealed with duct tape. Each one is a fire once and discard unit, and is equipped with a very simple but very accurate sight. Mariam stated that she had practiced using these units in Iraq and that they were very accurate out to several hundred meters.

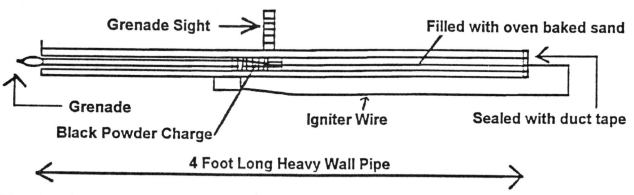

Grenade Sight →   **Filled with oven baked sand**

Grenade

Black Powder Charge   **Igniter Wire**   **Sealed with duct tape**

4 Foot Long Heavy Wall Pipe

When it comes time to deal with those high voltage step-up transformers, you simply put this over your shoulder, get your range (by holding out your thumb, looking at the target, closing one eye and seeing how far the landscape moves, put an imaginary post there, open that eye and close the other and see how far the landscape moves, put another imaginary post there, now judge the distance between the two imaginary posts as if you went out there and took a tape measure and measured it, then multiply that number by 9 which equals your range), set up your sight, and press the igniter. Equal blast goes out the back as is forcing the grenade forward, thus no recoil is felt. The inertial force holds the firing pin to the rear and allows the safety collar to slide back.

When the grenade plows into the transformer radiator, the sharp point pins the grenade in place, and the grenade stops. But inertia throws the firing pin forward, striking the shotshell primer. The primer detonates and ignites the double base powder producing a large number of high energy fragments, ripping the guts out of the radiator. Mariam stated that each cell was to be equipped with 20 of the above units. She then snickered and said "Made in America".

Mariam stated that she had no problem telling me all of this because "No one will ever believe you." She stated that she was on the move and probably would not see me again, and to please give her at least a week before I started making any inquiries for she knew that my curiosity would get the better of me. She closed her briefcase and got up and headed for the elevator, stopped and turned toward me and put out her hand and gestured like Spock from Star trek and said "Live long and prosper," She turned into the elevator and was gone.

A few days later I started a barrage of phone calls to the FBI, CDC, and just about anyone that I could think of to call. Mariam was right. No one believed me. Every bureaucrat that I called brushed me off. After an afternoon of phone tag with the CDC I finally was referred to Fort Collins, vector division. I divulged what Mariam had told me and they responded that they thought I had been watching too many science fiction movies and not to worry. I asked them if they had a contingency plan should something like this occur. They said that they did and I asked them if they would send me a copy of the plan. They said that they would.

After several weeks of waiting and no plan forthcoming more phone calls produced the finding that in 1972 all biological civil defense had been scrapped. There is no contingency plan. I just about flipped. They said "If you are a microbiologist and are so concerned why don't you write your own civil defense manual and leave us at the CDC alone."

My curiosity aroused and being sufficiently frustrated by official channels I opted to check out some of Mariam's assertions. I went first to the biological science building and sought one of the professors who was experienced with chemostats. He gave me several papers that verified what Mariam had said regarding chemostat operation. Next, I went to the Biological Science Library and obtained the information they had on plague. The librarian informed me that a visiting microbiologist who had written several papers on the dangers of germ warfare was going to deliver a lecture on his findings March 1993.

I attended the lecture, and after the questions from the audience I went forward to the speaker and introduced myself. I proposed we have a coffee in the small shop across from the library, and he accepted my offer. Over coffee I asked "What is the possibility of germ warfare becoming a threat to North America? And, if germ warfare is within the possibility of being acquired by a motivated and intelligent organization, why have we not seen it being used?

His response was that there is no cut and dry answer to this question! An explanation goes something like this: In the 1940's, when we began to look into the possibilities of using germ warfare, there were few, if any, antimicrobial drugs. So we had no way of really protecting our own troops. It was not until the later 1960's, when adequate antimicrobials had been developed, that the possibility of using biological warfare became a reality. However, about that time, it became apparent that just about any small country that could afford a laboratory could develop offensive weapons. At this point, the US Government started an active program of demonization of all aspects of biological warfare. This included cosponsoring the production of several movies: The Omega Man, The Virus, The Andromeda Strain, and others, to scare the hell out of the public. In 1972, this resulted in the United States signing the Convention on the Prohibition of the Development, Production and Stockpiling of Bacteriological and Toxin

Weapons and on their destruction. The US Government went on to glamorize those countries that possessed nuclear weapons, referring to it as the Nuclear Club. The strategy worked. Numerous small countries invested large portions of their defense budgets toward obtaining nuclear power. However, the Iraq war shocked many of these small countries into reality! They simply cannot afford to go nuclear. Bacteriological and biotoxin weapons they can afford. The lecturer stated very clearly -- **in the future we can almost certainly expect biological weapons to be used by various terrorist organizations.**

This makes it imperative that the citizens of North America obtain the necessary knowledge and skills to protect themselves against this emerging threat. Thus, the following book has been written to provide a source of information on aspects of biology having terrorist application. In addition, this book attempts to describe the types of biological agents that might be used against us, and how to defend against them.

CONTENTS

Chapter 1

Biological Warfare Defined
TM 3-216/AFM 355-6

Biological warfare is the military use of living organisms or their toxic products to cause death, disability, or damage to man, his domestic animals, or crops. Biological warfare agents include living organisms or their toxic products. The term "Germ warfare" or "Bacteriological warfare" is preferred to "Biological warfare" because it refers only to the use of bacteria. The technical procedures and equipment necessary for the recovery of toxic products produced by microorganisms is simply beyond the ability of most small countries and offer little advantage over living bacteria.

From the earliest time man has been continually fighting a defensive battle against microorganisms, in the form of disease, and has been able to survive through development of immunity, improvement in sanitation and nutrition, and the progress of medical science. The use of microorganisms as BW agents is simply a military adaptation of naturally occurring biological attacks. The suffering caused by most diseases is no greater than that caused by severe injuries by gun fire; the chances of complete recovery from infectious diseases are usually much greater than from injuries caused from other types of warfare. It has also been asserted by leading scientists that new, horrible diseases will be unleashed if BW occurs: this claim is true, as scientists working with the latest gene splicing techniques are producing some very dangerous diseases.

Several countries are genetically engineering viruses to be used in biological warfare. During the last few years medical science has been fighting an ever increasing number of laboratory created genetically "altered" viruses such as AIDS which by the very nature of their ability to continuously mutate, have resisted any kind of conventional medical treatment. It was created in military bio-labs for this purpose alone. And, only the military has the antidote. The individual that provided this information stated that he had numerous documents smuggled out of Wackenhut laboratories to confirm this fact.

For several weeks this writer communicated with a scientist who not only created these viruses, but owned a California corporation (Hercules Research Corporation) which developed them under contract for military applications. This scientist said he had files containing transcripts of conversations and backup documents relevant to those contracts. Any microbiologist familiar with today's technology knows the capabilities of these genetically altered, fast mutating viruses. They are certainly not naturally occurring and are far more lethal and less expensive to produce. This writer found out that back in the early 1980's some of this technology was sold to Iraq under the Reagan/Bush administration. If the virus happened to have been created in a laboratory, designed to mutate and destroy the body's T-cells, it cannot be treated in advance or even treated after infection if the body's immune system is the target. Most of these lab-created viruses attack the immune system first or the specific DNA of the individual.

The following is from research documents obtained from Wackenhut laboratories in which 20 African prostitutes in Nairobi and Gambia West Africa were used as research subjects by collaborating American, British and Japanese scientists to test the US Government's antidote against the "lab-created" HIV (AIDS) virus. The test was a huge success and all twenty of the

1

women NEVER contracted the HIV virus after being exposed consistently for five years. The reason, their Cytotoxic T - Lymphocytes (CTL's) or T-Cells were raised to extremely high levels by the injected antidote.

The following are excerpts from one of these documents:

" . . . the sera of the prostitutes showed that the women were generating highly specific cytotoxic T - Lymphocyte (CTL) responses to both HIV-1 and HIV-2 peptides. The HIV-specific CTLs were studied utilizing peptides epitopes which are bound in MHC (major hisocompatability complex) molecules on the surface of the infected cells and presented to the T-Cell receptors of the CTL . . . "

" . . . The finding of HIV - specific CTL, **able to kill virus-infected cells**, in uninfected but repeatedly HIV-exposed women, indicated that the PCR serum developed antibodies in the subjects over a three month period. The protective immunity developed against HIV in all 20 women emphasized the vaccine's ability to utilize cytotoxic T - lymphocytes to retain CD-4 cell counts above 500 with no symptomatic viremic responses over a five-year period . . ."

A study group of HIV-infected mothers in Nairobi were also given the serum and gave birth to HIV-free babies. And a subgroup of HIV-exposed US men were given the vaccine and have shown no signs or symptoms of "any" disease for over five years.

In other words, not only has biological technology been created to destroy an individual's immune system, as evidenced by rampant emerging "new" diseases in targeted areas worldwide, but technology exists today in government sponsored laboratories to "increase" the immune system 100% against "lab-created" viruses.

The HIV (AIDS) virus is a RACO Race Specific Organism, in that is was designed to kill only Negroes. The HIV virus was placed into serum (some say smallpox) and inoculated into Negroes for their removal from Africa. The HIV virus was designed to use an intermediate bacterial carrier, that is present in a Negro's body but not present in Caucasians. This strategy has been extremely effective and by some estimates the Negro population of Africa will soon be reduced to below 5 million.

Because naturally occurring epidemics have caused tremendous havoc to mankind in the past, it has been asserted frequently that artificially induced epidemics could be produced in the future by attack with various biological agents. However, since epidemics tend to spread slowly, they probably can be effectively controlled or prevented by modern sanitation, hygiene, quarantine, immunization, or treatment measures; hence, widespread explosive epidemics are not expected to result from BW attacks against highly civilized populations <u>unless there has been severe disruption of medical and sanitary facilities, and a massive attack carried out simultaneously across the country.</u>

It is true that BW attacks the noncombatant populations as well as the Armed Forces. This is equally true of attack on a city by aircraft or by artillery. Destruction or incapacitation of a significant portion of civilian personnel in a given situation also might be a desired factor if the target was a financial hub, like Wall Street (recently the Stock Market had an outbreak of Tuberculosis, now every broker that trades on the stock exchange must be tested) or The World Trade Center. In such event, cities, factories, and homes, and other attributes of civilization would not be destroyed, and rehabilitation would be much more easily effected than after conventional bombing attacks.

BACTERIOLOGICAL WARFARE

Although germ warfare has never been used yet as a significant weapon of war, there is factual evidence that they have been used in some form since early times. In the middle ages war parties dropped plague-ridden corpses into wells of their enemy. This type of warfare was practiced particularly in desert warfare where wells were of strategic importance and easily contaminated. During the French and Indian War, 1763, the British infected the Indians with smallpox by giving them blankets and handkerchiefs taken from infected patients. Approximately 95% of the Indians that were exposed died of the disease. In World War I German agents inoculated horses and cattle shipped from the United States to the Allies with disease producing bacteria. (The Germans used glanders against the Rumanian Cavalry.) In 1940, claims were made by the Chinese that Japanese planes had dropped plague infected fleas wrapped in little cotton bags containing grain. It was assumed that their purpose was to initiate an epidemic of plague by utilizing their natural vectors. In the past, widespread natural disease epidemics have decimated the populations of various areas. In many wars, infection and disease have caused more casualties than have weapons.

Since BW has never been used as a weapon of war on a major scale, no definite evaluation can be made of its effectiveness. The fact that very little is known of the potential tactical or strategic value of BW in modern warfare should not lead to an underestimation of its possibilities. It has been established that BW agents can be produced on a scale not considered possible in the past. Any small nation having modern and adequate research facilities could produce BW agents on a small scale. The cost of the development of large-scale BW would be much less than that incident to some other weapons of war. It is also possible that new and effective methods for artificial dissemination of disease producing agents may be developed. For these reasons, BW must be assumed to present a potentially dangerous form of attack, especially for the Middle Eastern countries, whose agenda includes terrorism. It is possible that within the next decade many parts of the North American continent could be turned into disease infested hell holes. Some basic knowledge of the principles of biology and of the properties of biological agents is essential for the appreciation of their military significance, so that preparations can be made by the citizens of North America to render a Terrorist BW attack as ineffective as possible when they occur.

Five general groups have been classed as BW agents because they appear to have military significance. However, we will consider only microorganisms, bacteria and viruses because these are the ones that can cause the greatest harm, making them the logical choice for groups bent on terrorism. Mariam Arif stated that Iraq planned to use only bacteria against the United States . A designer virus is too unpredictable. Mariam stated that Iraq had done extensive research in order to design a RACO that would kill only Caucasians and not Iraqis, but they could not find a single intermediate bacterial carrier that Caucasians had and Iraqis did not have. Also anthrax and plague can be easily isolated from nature, are more deadly than an atomic bomb and, with some antibiotics, their agents would not get the disease. And they love the sweet irony of buying it from the Americans, and then using it on them.

Chapter 2

Microorganisms
TM 3-216/AFM 355-6

2 - 1 Characteristics of Microorganisms

Microorganisms are minute living organisms, usually microscopic, that is, too small to be seen by the unaided eye. When magnified 500 to 1000 times by the microscope each microorganism is found to be composed of a single cell or a group of associated cells, each of which is capable of carrying on all the functions of life including growth and reproduction. Lacking a digestive tract the microorganism acquires food in soluble form through the moist membrane that surrounds the cell contents. Not possessing organs of sight, it does not differentiate light and darkness by the visual method. Having no heat regulating system it assumes the temperature of its surroundings. Microorganisms are so small that the unit applied in their measurement is the micron, which is equivalent to 0.001 millimeter or approximately 1/25,000 of an inch.

Microorganisms capable of producing disease are called pathogens. Most of the pathogens are parasites since they live in, on, or with some other living host at whose expense they obtain food and shelter. Organisms that multiply in dead, rather than in living matter, are called saprophytes. While most of these are harmless, some produce poisonous products that cause disease. Examples of some of these harmful saprophytes are the bacteria that cause tetanus, producing their poison in macerated, devitalized tissue, and those that cause botulism, manufacturing their toxin in food outside the body.

Most microorganisms are nonpathogenic, and many are beneficial to animal and plant life. From the secretions of certain microorganisms some of the most powerful antibiotics, such as chloromycetin, penicillin, and streptomycin, have been obtained. Microorganisms are important in the preparation of dairy products and in the fermentation industry (for example, rising of bread and production of vinegar and alcoholic beverages). Soil fertility is largely dependent upon their activity in decomposing dead matter and releasing the elements needed for the growth of plants.

Microorganisms are universally distributed in the air, water, and soil. Soil organisms are found in all surface exposed to dirt and dust, and every cubic foot of topsoil provides the natural home for billions of them. The skin, hair, nose, mouth, and digestive tract of man and animals harbor a considerable variety of microorganisms in large numbers. However, the pathogenic, or disease-producing organisms of man, animals, and plants, with very few exceptions, usually do not survive long or grow well without a suitable host, and favorable environmental conditions are necessary for their survival.

2 - 2 Growth and Survival

Numerous factors influence the growth of microorganisms, which are more dependent on a delicately adjusted environment than are higher forms of life. Some of their requirements are presented below.

BACTERIOLOGICAL WARFARE

MOISTURE.

A plentiful supply of water is essential, as this amounts to about nine-tenths of the cellular substance, and is the vehicle by means of which soluble food is made available by diffusion through the cell wall. It also is required in the immediate surroundings to prevent drying of the organism; even a small decrease may interfere with normal functions and cause death. However, it is possible to keep even quite delicate organisms alive by lyophilization, which is a combined process of quick freezing and drying at very low temperatures.

FOOD.

Food is required to supply building material and energy. Microorganisms in general can utilize a wide variety of substances, including proteins, sugars, minerals, salts, and vitamins, but the requirements of different species are not the same, either in the kinds of foods or in their proportions. As mentioned previously, the parasites normally feed on living plants or animals but, under favorable conditions, some will grow in foodstuffs or artificial media, the saprophytes require dead or decaying organic matter. The viruses and rickettsiae will grow only in the presence of living host cells, thus they are obligate parasites.

OXYGEN.

As with higher forms of life, all microorganisms require oxygen to live, but they may differ markedly regarding the source from which they obtain it. Those which grow only in the presence of free oxygen are called obligate aerobes, while those which grow only in the absence of free oxygen are termed obligate anaerobes and obtain their oxygen in the combined form from various chemical compounds. Between these two extremes are the facultative aerobes, which are fundamentally anaerobes but can grow in the presence of free oxygen, and the facultative anaerobes, which are essentially aerobes but can grow in the absence of free oxygen. Most of the pathogenic microorganisms are facultative because they may obtain their oxygen in either form. In either case, the supply of oxygen is essential to provide energy and to aid in the formation of new cellular material.

TEMPERATURE.

Temperature is an important factor, each species of organism developing most abundantly at a particular or optimum temperature range. Pathogens of warm-blooded animals develop best in the narrow temperature ranges common to these animals. At variations either below or above this range, the organism functions progressively less effectively until temperatures are reached at which growth no longer occurs. High temperatures are fatal, but survival often occurs at low temperatures. Climatic conditions might be decisive factors in determining whether certain microorganisms could be used in desert or Arctic warfare.

LIGHT.

Most microorganisms do not require light for growth. They are destroyed by prolonged direct exposure to ultraviolet rays from the sun or from artificial sources. Consequently growth occurs best in the dark, or at least in an environment protected from direct sunlight.

REACTION OF MEDIUM.

In general, most microorganisms associated with animal life grow best in neutral or slightly alkaline surroundings, while those associated with plant life often prefer a slightly acid environment. Growth is inhibited by either highly acid or highly alkaline surroundings.

TIME.

When microorganisms are placed in a new environment, there is a period of adjustment or lag phase in which the number of cells does not increase appreciably. If all essential factors are favorable and there is no opposition from the host, an insignificant number of organisms may develop within a few hours, or at most, days, into numbers almost beyond comprehension.

ENCAPSULATION.

The formation of capsules, a process known as encapsulation, is a property of many bacteria that may favor their survival. The capsule is also associated with a variety of pathogenic bacteria. For example, pneumococci that are encapsulated are highly virulent whereas when they have no capsule they are relatively avirulent. ANTHRAX bacilli are almost always found to be encapsulated when observed in preparations made from animal tissues. The capsule appears to function as a bacterial defense against the activity of phagocytic cells of the body. The capsule apparently originates from the outer layer of the cell membrane and consists of a thick, colorless (translucent) outer wall of gelatinous (protein), gummy (polysaccharide), or fatty material. There is good reason to believe that capsule formation may be stimulated by unfavorable environmental conditions such as the resistance of an infected host.

SPORULATION.

Another protective mechanism favorable to survival among bacteria is sporulation, which leads to the formation of heavy walled bodies called spores. Sporulation is not necessarily a response to unfavorable conditions, since spores are often formed early in the life of a culture while conditions are wholly favorable to continued vegetative activity. Bacterial spores are more resistant to injurious or unfavorable influences (such as starvation, high and low temperatures, germicidal chemicals, drying, and oxidation) than the growing or vegetative forms. When the spore has matured, the surrounding vegetative form disintegrates. The resistant spores thus formed may remain dormant for years without food or water, and under extreme range of temperatures, and again develop into an actively growing vegetative cell when conditions become favorable. Spore formation is not a method of multiplication in the bacteria. Each vegetative cell form only a single spore and each spore will germinate into a single vegetative cell. Therefore, it is considered a means for the perpetuation of the organism. Since the rate of growth of certain species is accelerated after spore formation, the process may serve to rejuvenate the activities of the bacterial cell. In higher fungi, such as molds and mushrooms, spore formation, either sexual or asexual, is the normal method of reproduction.

2 - 3 Reproduction

Reproduction may be sexual or asexual, depending on the microorganism, but the asexual process is the more common.

ASEXUAL.

Asexual reproduction may occur by binary fission, by budding, or sporulation. In binary fission, the cell divides into two equal and identical parts, each of which develops into a new organism. In budding, a small portion of the parent cell is pinched off and develops into a new, actively growing individual. In fungal sporulation, special cells are set aside for reproduction. The bacteria reproduce by asexual binary fission; the yeasts, which belong to the fungi, reproduce sometimes by asexual binary fission but usually by budding or by sexual spore formation. The higher fungi usually reproduce by sporulation. Protozoa may reproduce by fission, but sexual reproduction is common in certain species.

SEXUAL.

Sexual methods of reproduction are often encountered among microorganisms. These involve copulation of two cells with interchange of cellular contents, usually resulting in the formation of spores of various types. Sexual reproduction is known to occur among the fungi and protozoa, although it is often difficult to identify the cells as male or female.

2 - 4 Identification

The methods involved in the identification of most microorganisms are difficult and time consuming and usually are dependent upon obtaining living organisms. Organisms exhibit preference for environments in which they will grow (that is, the type of material required for their survival). Information as to the source of the organism is of value in establishing its identity. Usually, such information will not be available under conditions of BW. Laboratory procedures are used to establish or confirm the identity of a microorganism. A few of these methods are described below.

SAMPLING.

Rapid identification of a microorganism used as a BW Agent is dependent upon sampling procedures capable of obtaining a large number of viable organisms relatively free from interfering materials or other organisms. Methods of collecting suspected material vary with its nature and source, that is, living or dead tissue, body secretions, soil, air, water, surfaces of all kinds, and with methods of its release, such as aerosols from various spraying devices or bombs. If the agent is released as an aerosol (cloud or spray), every effort should be made to obtain an air sample as near the point of release as possible. The number as well as the viability of the organisms released in an aerosol will decrease progressively with the passage of time and with increasing distance from the point of release outward. Also the original aerosol is relatively uncontaminated, since there are few naturally occurring organisms in the air. Samples of vegetation, water, soil, and other materials on which the agent has fallen may be of value in aiding or helping confirm the identity of the agent even though the samples contain interfering contamination and yield a smaller number of organisms than are found in the original aerosol. Such samples should be taken if conditions or other factors make it impossible to obtain air samples of the original aerosol or if there is evidence that a poorly representative sample might have been taken. These samples should be taken as soon after release and as near the point of release as possible. Air samples may be obtained by drawing the air through a simple coffee filter, or bubblers, by bringing the air in contact with the surface of nutrient media, or by using special filtering devices. Vegetation, water, and soil samples are obtained by placing portions of each in sterile containers. Samples from other contaminated surfaces may be obtained by rubbing the surface with a sterile cotton swab and placing in a sterile capped container. The samples are then sent, by the fastest method available, to the nearest designated laboratory for identification.

MICROSCOPIC EXAMINATION.

Microorganisms (except viruses and rickettsiae) in smears or suspensions of suspected material may be examined and counted under a microscope for identification purposes. Such examinations may be aided by staining the microorganisms with dyes, which bring into sharper detail the shape, relative size, and presence of spores, capsules, or flagella of certain microorganisms that otherwise might not be noted. A very important staining procedure is the Gram method. In this process the specimens are first stained, then exposed to a decolorizing fluid, and subsequently counterstained. Organisms retaining the primary stain are called gram positive, and those stained by the secondary stain are gram negative.

CULTURE.

Microorganisms may be cultivated by placing samples of them in sterile containers holding solid or liquid nutrient media and incubating them at temperatures suitable for growth for specific lengths of time. Organisms multiplying on solid media form visible masses or colonies whose surface appearance, shape, and color help in their identification. In liquid media, identification of the microorganism is aided by determining what kinds of food are required for its growth and what substances it produces.

TESTS.

Microorganisms may be identified biochemically by cultivation of them in certain media, observation of the byproducts of their growth, and determination of what materials they consume. By the addition of certain chemical compounds to the media, it is possible also to differentiate between different kinds of microorganisms by unequally influencing their growth. Biological tests are also useful for identifying many microorganisms. Suitable animals are injected with the suspected organism, and clinical or postmortem observations of pathological changes are made. When a certain kind of organism is under suspicion, it may be inoculated into animals that have been immunized against it and into an equal number of nonimmunized animals; if the suspicion is correct, the nonimmunized animals will develop the disease, while the immunized animals will not. A third method of identification is by serological testing. This is based upon the occurrence in all living cells of specific protein substances known as antigens that, when introduced into the blood or tissue of a foreign animal body, induce the formation of specifically reacting antagonistic substances known as antibodies. Since antibodies usually appear in the blood serum, which is then used in testing for specific antigens, these antigen-antibody reactions are known as serological reactions. It is possible with serological reactions to distinguish between different but closely related organisms, thus aiding in the diagnosing of an infectious disease.

2 - 5 Inhibition and Destruction

The term "inhibition" is used to indicate arrest in growth or multiplication (reproduction), while destruction refers to death; sterilization is synonymous with destruction. These phenomena may be brought about by physical, chemical, or biological means.

TEMPERATURE.

High temperatures are effective in destroying microorganisms. Higher temperatures or longer exposures are required when dry heat is used than when moist heat is used. Direct exposure to flame and to steam under pressure is reliable for sterilizing materials that are not harmed by these methods. Boiling water or flowing steam is effective when resistant species or spores are absent. Some delicate organisms, however, do not survive even small temperature fluctuations of their environment. On the other hand, rapid lowering of the temperature to subfreezing accompanied by quick drying tends to preserve the life of many microorganisms, and they survive in a state of suspended animation.

DESICCATION.

Desiccation, or drying, is one of the oldest measures used to prevent spoilage of food by microorganisms, examples being the production of jerked beef, prunes, powdered milk and eggs, and other dehydrated foods. Without moisture, food cannot diffuse through the cell membrane, and growth of the organism ceases. Vegetative organisms are particularly susceptible to drying, but spores are practically unharmed. Drying may reduce the number of living organisms but cannot be relied upon for their complete destruction.

STARVATION.

Growth can be inhibited and sometimes death induced when essential food materials are removed or rendered unavailable. All microorganisms require oxygen, carbon, nitrogen, and hydrogen in some form; if any one of these elements is limited or converted to an unusable form, the microorganism cannot develop and may eventually die. Varying amounts of other materials too numerous to name in this text also are essential, depending on the kind of organism involved. Spores, as opposed to vegetative forms, can remain dormant for long periods without food; hence spores may not be killed by starvation, but their germination may be prevented.

LIGHT.

Ultraviolet rays from the sun or artificial sources quickly destroy exposed microorganisms, but these rays have low penetrating powers and may be ineffective against microbes protected by thin liquid or dust films, rough surfaces, or opaque liquids.

FILTRATION.

Microorganisms can be removed from air and liquids by various filtering devices. The efficiency of filtering processes depends not only on the kind of filter used but also upon such factors as particle size and number of organisms present, electrostatic charge, and rapidity of filtration. The larger organisms may be removed by filtration through asbestos pads, colloidal or other specially prepared membranes, filter paper, or unglazed porcelain, the pore sizes of which are too small to permit passage of the microorganisms. Some microorganisms, such as viruses, are so small that they cannot be removed by ordinary bacterial filters but require special filtration devices. Gases such as air, containing dust like suspensions of microorganisms, can be effectively filtered through thick layers of cotton batting or other materials.

OSMOSIS.

The diffusion of a liquid through a semipermeable membrane that separates two miscible solutions is known as osmosis. Although the diffusion may proceed in both directions, the flow of solvent is greater from the more dilute to the more concentrated solution. This diffusion tends to equalize the concentration of the two solutions. Osmotic pressure is the increased pressure that develops in the more highly concentrated solution. Living cells, including microorganisms, all have semipermeable cell membranes. When they are placed in high sugar or salt concentrations, the osmotic process removes water from them, resulting in inhibition of growth or destruction. Common applications of this principle are the use of high concentrations of sugar or preserve foods, such as jams and jellies, and the soaking of meat in brine. However, these measures are not effective for destroying spores.

2 - 6 Chemical

GENERAL.

Many chemical compounds are used to destroy or inhibit the growth of microorganisms. Disinfectants are materials such as germicides and bactericides, which destroy pathogenic microorganisms. Antiseptics are substances that inhibit the growth and development of microorganisms, but do not necessarily destroy them. Some chemicals are powerful disinfectants, while others are only inhibitors. Among the common disinfectant and antiseptic preparations are mercuric chloride, silver nitrate, tincture of iodine, chlorine, phenol, cresol, formaldehyde, hydrogen peroxide, alcohol, hypochlorites, and acids or alkalies. The vapors of

propylene glycol, triethylene glycol, and ethylene oxide are also effective disinfectants and decontaminants. Proper concentration, temperature, and length of exposure are critical factors in the employment of all these materials.
CHEMOTHERAPEUTIC AGENTS.

These are chemical compounds, used in the treatment of disease. They affect the causative microorganism unfavorably without markedly injuring the patient. They may destroy the pathogen, inhibit its growth, or render it more susceptible to the defense mechanisms of the body. Among these substances are the arsphenamines, quinine, and the sulfonamides-sulfanilamide, sulfadiazine, and sulfapyridine and others.

2 - 7 Biological
ANTIBIOTICS.

Are substances (chemical compounds) produced by living cells and are selectively antagonistic to other living organisms. (They have the capacity to inhibit the growth of and to destroy various microorganisms.) Antibiotics are usually obtained from microorganisms, such as bacteria, yeasts, and molds, and sometimes from higher plants. Some antibiotics originally obtained from a microorganism, such as chloromycetin, have been synthesized. No one antibiotic is inhibitory to all microorganisms, but each has a reasonably specific inhibitory or growth preventing action on particular species. Some have proved valuable in the treatment of diseases not responsive to chemotheraputic drugs, vaccines, or antiserums. Prominent antibiotics include penicillin, streptomycin, chloromycetin, and terramycin.
BACTERIOPHAGES.

Are viruses that are parasitic to certain bacteria and may destroy them. Like other viruses, bacteriophages multiply only in the presence of living cells. They are widely distributed in nature and are commonly present in the intestines of man and animals, especially those recovering from a bacterial disease. There are various strains or races of bacteriophage, each being specific for certain types or groups of bacteria, but many bacteria, including some of the more pathogenic, have no known bacteriophage. A very small amount of bacteriophage, when added to an actively growing susceptible bacterial culture, will cause swelling, death, and disintegration of the bacterial cells within a few hours.

2 - 8 Infection and Immunity
GENERAL.

Infection occurs when pathogenic microorganisms invade the tissue, multiply, and produce injury or death. It represents a conflict between the invader and the living object of attack in which the host strives to resist the invasion and repel the invading organisms. If they are repelled, the defender suffers no ill effects; if not, infection occurs. Factors that influence the outcome of the struggle are the PORTALS OF ENTRY, THE VIRULENCE AND NUMBER OF ORGANISMS, AND THE DEFENSE POWERS OF THE DEFENDER - MAN, ANIMAL, OR PLANT. Microorganisms range from those which produce disease (pathogens) to those which do not produce disease (nonpathogens). Under some circumstances, organisms that are considered nonpathogenic may produce infections; examples are the normal bacteria of the gastrointestinal tract which can produce disease like peritonitis, colitis, and urinary tract infections. Infections may or may not be transmissible to other individuals; a contagious disease is an infection that spreads readily from one individual to another by direct or indirect contact.

BACTERIOLOGICAL WARFARE

Typhoid fever, Plague, Anthrax, and Cholera are major agents of germ warfare. The chief requirement of an effective biological weapon is that the organism be highly infectious by the respiratory route, thus permitting effective airborne dispersal. Plague (Yersinia pestis) and Anthrax are the most likely candidates a terrorist would use against the North American Continent. These organisms are highly infectious and cause a serious incapacitating disease that is often fatal. The organism can infect either the respiratory or oral route, and can be readily cultivated in the laboratory. All contagious diseases are infectious; however, infectious diseases are not necessarily contagious (tetanus, brucellosis, tularemia, malaria).

2 - 9 Factors of Infection
VIRULENCE.

Virulence refers to the relative infectiousness of an organism or its ability to overcome the defenses of the host. Pathogens range in virulence from those producing mild and temporary disturbances to those causing incapacitation or death. Virulence of certain organisms can be increased by repeated passage from animal to animal. In general, virulence is dependent on two factors -- invasiveness and toxicity.
INVASIVENESS.

Invasiveness is the ability of a microorganism to enter the body and spread through the tissue. It is the predominant factor in the virulence of some microorganisms, such as those causing tularemia and blood poisoning.
INFECTIVE DOSE.

The infective dose denotes the number of organisms necessary to produce infection in an exposed individual. It is an extremely variable factor. Depending on the microorganism involved and the species or individual attacked relatively few organisms can produce an infection, while in others large numbers may be repelled by the body.
INCUBATION PERIOD.

After microorganisms have been introduced into the host in sufficient amounts to produce disease, an interval of time, known as the incubation period, elapses before symptoms of disease appear. During this time the organisms establish themselves firmly and increase in numbers large enough to cause disease. The incubation period may vary from a few hours to a few weeks, depending on the kind of pathogen and, during this interval, there may be no sign of disease. At the end of the period, symptoms may appear either gradually or suddenly, and the fully developed disease will become evident. A similar lapse of time occurs between the introduction of non-living toxins and the appearance of disease symptoms; they may more aptly be termed a latent, rather than an incubation period.
ROUTES OF INFECTION.

The principal portals of entry for microorganisms into man and animals are through ABRASIONS OF THE SKIN, THROUGH THE MUCOUS MEMBRANES OF THE RESPIRATORY, GASTROINTESTINAL, AND GENITOURINARY TRACTS, AND THROUGH THE EYE. However, it should be recognized that the unbroken skin and mucous membranes are natural defense barriers which aid in preventing an invasion by pathogenic organisms. Certain organisms require specific routes to infect, while others can invade by several routes. Most respiratory diseases are contracted by the inhalation of droplets of contaminated moisture or dust. Intestinal infections are produced by the ingestion of contaminated food or drink. Some organisms invade by penetration of the skin through hair follicles, sweat gland ducts, or abrasions; other organisms must enter through wounds to establish themselves. Tetanus spores, for example, may be swallowed with impunity by man; but if they are introduced into a lacerated wound, tetanus may develop.

SYMPTOMS OF INFECTION.

In the early stage of disease, a few general symptoms usually appear which indicate that infection has been established. These are FEVER, MALAISE, and INFLAMMATION.

FEVER.

Warm-blooded animals, including man, normally maintain their body temperatures within quite narrow limits. The occurrence of an infection usually is accomplished by an abnormal rise in temperature, which is called fever. The degree of fever varies in different diseases, but may serve as a rough guide to the severity of the infection; however, the rise in temperature is a protective mechanism, unless it gets so high that it is harmful to the patient. As a rule, the individual with fever feels quite warm and his skin is likely to be flushed. The onset of fever may be preceded by chill that causes him to shiver, sometimes violently. The chill does not necessarily indicate a drop in body temperature, even though there is a cooling sensation of the skin; the temperature of the interior of the body may be abnormally high. Fever, whether preceded by a chill or not, is usually one of the earliest symptoms of infection and is indicative of illness.

MALAISE.

This is another early set of symptoms of infection in which there is a vague feeling of bodily discomfort, weakness, and exhaustion. It may be accompanied by nausea, dizziness, loss of appetite, and generalized aches. Pains in the back, arms, legs, and head may be present as well. These symptoms may increase in severity as the disease develops or may be overshadowed by other specific symptoms.

INFLAMMATION.

Inflammation is a reaction of certain body tissues to injury and is characterized by pain, heat, redness, and swelling. Certain kinds of infection are indicated by inflammation of the skin, mucous membranes, or glands, as the body defenses are mobilized to combat the invader and seal off the infection. Some infections are accompanied by a characteristic eruption or rash of the skin, by means of which it is often possible to make an early diagnosis of the particular type of infection that has occurred.

2 - 10 Resistance to Infection

The ability of the body to fight off or overcome an infection is known as resistance. The first line of defense is provided by the skin and mucous membranes of the gastrointestinal, respiratory, and genitourinary tracts, and their secretions. These help prevent entrance of microorganisms into deeper tissues, which have little ability to ward off invasion. The second line of defense, of which the lymphatic system is a part, is a cellular one, in which specific migrating cells of the body attack and destroy the invading organisms. The third line of defense is presented by the blood, which contains neutralizing bodies, and the liver and spleen, to which the blood carries organisms and toxins to be destroyed or inactivated.

THE SKIN AND MUCOUS MEMBRANES.

The unbroken skin and mucous membranes act as mechanical barriers and are generally impervious to particulate material of bacterial size, some of which may, however, enter the skin through hair follicles and sweat gland ducts. Clean skin is also actively bactericidal to many pathogenic microorganisms. Sweat acts as a bactericide and also aids in flushing away the germs. The mucous membrane, or mucosa, lines the surface of the canals and cavities of the body which communicate with the exterior, such as the alimentary canal and its connections, the respiratory tract and its branches, and the genitourinary tract. The mucosa produces a viscid watery secretion, known as mucus, which forms a protective covering and entangles invading microorganisms. The constant movement, or peristalsis, of the gastrointestinal tract tends to trap microorganisms in shreds of mucus and thus passes the organism into the lower bowel and out of the body. Microorganisms are also entangled by the mucus of the nasal passages and trachea, or windpipe, and swept back to the mouth by coughing or by the action of cilia, which are small hairlike projections lining these surfaces. The mucus of the genitourinary tract acts in a similar manner. Other secretions, such as the acid juices of the stomach, the alkaline ones of the intestines, and the vaginal secretions, either inhibit or destroy microorganisms, and the saliva and tears protect the body by a combination of lyasome and mechanical flushing.

CELLULAR DEFENSE.

Should microorganisms succeed in gaining entrance into deeper tissues, they are attacked by cells known as phagocytes, which appear at the site of invasion within a few minutes and have the ability to ingest and destroy foreign bodies in the blood and other tissues. If the infective agents overwhelm the phagocytes and penetrate more deeply, they may enter the lymph channels and be carried to the lymph nodes where they are engulfed by larger phagocytes. The swelling and tenderness of the lymph nodes are symptoms of this struggle.

BLOOD DEFENSE.

In addition to the white blood cells, or leucocytes, which are wandering phagocytes, the blood also contains substances called antibodies. These are immune bodies manufactured by the body in response to the introduction of antigens, foreign protein like substances, into the tissues. Vaccines are typical antigens which, when injected into the body, cause antibodies to be formed. Microorganisms and their products, such as toxins, are protein in nature; hence they are antigens. Each antibody is specifically antagonistic to the antigen which stimulated its production and combines with the antigen to neutralize or destroy it. Many kinds of antibodies are the basis of the active immunity which may be induced naturally or artificially in the body to provide resistance against invading microorganisms or their poisonous products. Should the invading microorganisms overcome the cellular and blood defenses, they are carried into the blood stream and attacked by the large white cells or macrophages in the liver, spleen, and bone marrow, where the blood flow is slower then in other parts of the body, allowing more time and greater opportunity for the macrophages to engulf them.

2 - 11 Immunity

GENERAL.

The ability of the living individual to resist or overcome infection or injury by a pathogenic agent is known as immunity. Relative resistance to infection is dependent upon all the protective barriers, including the skin, mucous membranes, tissue cells, and blood. Resistance due to the presence of certain antibodies in the tissue is the primary factor in determining an individual's immunity. Immunity may be classified into several types.

NATURAL IMMUNITY.

Certain species of animals, CERTAIN RACES OF PEOPLE, and certain individuals of a given race appear to be born with a resistance to certain infections. Examples of natural immunity are the resistance of man to foot-and-mouth disease, the resistance of dogs to anthrax, and the relative resistance of the Negro race to yellow fever.

ACQUIRED IMMUNITY.

This type of immunity may be either naturally or artificially acquired and may be active or passive.

* NATURALLY ACQUIRED PASSIVE IMMUNITY (congenital) infants possess immunity to certain infections in the first months of life due to antibodies acquired from the mother. These antibodies soon disappear, and the conferred immunity is then lost. An example of this type of immunity is the resistance of infants to diphtheria during the first year of life.

* NATURALLY ACQUIRED ACTIVE IMMUNITY. This type of immunity is generally the longest lasting of all immunities. It may be the result of recovery from an attack of an infectious diseases such as typhoid, diphtheria, or tularemia (rabbit fever); or may be attributed to an earlier, mild, unrecognized infection or to repeated contact with the disease producing organism in insufficient quantities to produce disease.

* ARTIFICIALLY ACQUIRED ACTIVE IMMUNITY. This type of immunity is produced through injection of vaccines of attenuated or dead organisms or injection of toxoids (inactivated toxins) to which the body reacts by forming specific antibodies. Duration of immunity thus acquired varies considerably, depending upon the specific disease and the type of vaccine or toxoid used. Examples of effective vaccines are those of smallpox and typhoid. An example of an effective toxoid is that of diphtheria.

* ARTIFICIALLY ACQUIRED PASSIVE IMMUNITY. This type of immunity is obtained by the injection into the body of antibodies (immune serum) actively produced in another individual or animal in response to either natural infection or injections of specific vaccines. An example of this is the immunity conferred by an injection of tetanus antitoxin. This immunity is relatively short lived.

TREATMENT PROBLEMS.

Certain factors may arise in a terrorism germ attack that will complicate treatment of casualties. These factors include the probable employment of overwhelming numbers of pathogenic organisms in an attack, AND THE UNAVAILABILITY OF SUFFICIENT QUALITIES OF ANTIBIOTIC, AND SHORTAGES OF MEDICAL SUPPLIES, PERSONNEL AND FACILITIES, due to an overwhelming number of casualties occurring at one time. Other complicating factors might include fatigue, malnutrition, and climate conditions which would accelerate the course and severity of the resulting disease.

2 - 12 Vectors of Disease

In general, the term "vector" refers to the arthropods, including such insects as mosquitoes, flies, fleas, and lice, and a few acarids, such as mites and ticks. In some cases higher animals such as rats, cats, dogs and even man himself are considered vectors.

FLIES.

The true flies have only two wings, but the word "fly" is often applied in compound names of other insects, such as mayfly, saw fly, and stonefly. Most of the many varieties of flies have sucking mouth parts, but those few which have mouth structures capable of piercing the skin of man or animals include the most important disease vectors. The sucking flies can, however, introduce infection through previously injured body surfaces and are capable of mechanically transferring pathogens to exposed surfaces and food. TYPHOID FEVER Bacillary and amoebic dysentery, and CHOLERA are examples of disease which may be spread mechanically by nonbiting flies. Yaws, a highly infectious and contagious nonveneral spirochetal disease resembling syphilis, may be acquired through a cut or abrasion of the skin, either directly by contact with discharges from lesions or indirectly through the agency of nonbiting flies. The nonbiting flies, which include the common housefly, are often termed "filth flies"; it should be emphasized that they easily may carry pathogenic microorganisms from excrement, sputum, open sores, or putrefying matter of food, milk, and healthy mucous membranes. Tularemia (rabbit fever), is a bacterial disease of wild animals and man sometimes transmitted by the horsefly and wood tick.

FLEAS.

Fleas are small, wingless, insect parasites of the skin of mammals and birds. Their bodies are flattened laterally, and they have mouth parts for piercing the skin. While different species show preferences for certain hosts, when hungry they will attack any warm-blooded animals, which greatly increases their potential to transmit disease to man. The common rat flea is the vector of marine typhus, a rickettsial disease of rats and mice, and occasionally bites and infects man with the disease; it is the chief vector of PLAGUE from rats and other rodents to man and among rats and mice. Other fleas are known vectors of PLAGUE in the western United States. Fleas can also transmit HIV (AIDS).

LICE.

The lice are sucking, dorso-ventrally flattened, wingless insects, parasitic on the skin of mammals and birds. The body louse (and probably the head louse) is the vector of rickettsial diseases, epidemic typhus, trench fever, PLAGUE and HIV (AIDS).

Chapter 3

General Properties of Biological Warfare Agents
TM 3-216/AFM 355-6

3 - 1 Purpose

The purpose of using BW agents is to produce widespread injury or death in man. Under the term "living organisms" are included not only microorganisms, but also higher forms of animal life which injure by acting as vectors of disease. The microorganisms which could be used as BW agents are few compared with the total number known. Any pathogen that could cause a disease having high mortality or morbidity rates might be useful in Biological Warfare. Although toxins are comparatively scarce in number, they include some of the most poisonous substances known. Practical problems exist which have to be solved before their potential usefulness can be realized. The former Soviet Union, after an enormous out lay of capital, came up with an effective biotoxin weapon. This weapon was known by the term "yellow rain". the production process involves the solvent extraction of a toxin produced by Staphylococci aureus which causes Disseminated Intravascular Coagulation. This toxin was impregnated upon wheat flower giving a yellow color. This material had to be maintained in an oxygen free environment prior to being used, as oxygen would deactivate the toxin within 48 hours. The toxin was delivered to targets primarily in two ways, one way was to spray it from aircraft over a target area. The toxin settled on the ground in a yellow mist, thus the term "yellow rain"; the lethal dose was very small. Once inhaled, the blood started to coagulate from the head and lungs. Death resulted within minutes, and as the toxin was deactivated within forty eight hours, soldiers could quickly and safely enter the area. This toxin weapon was also mounted onto RPG's for selected targets. Another biotoxin developed by the former Soviet Union was the STAR, this was pure crystalline Botulism toxin and is the most powerful poison known. It was believed to be a sabotage weapon, to be directed against domestic water supplies. It is unknown how far this project went, or if it was even completed. If indeed this project was completed and a terrorist group obtained this weapon, the introduction into a city's water supply would cause an enormous death toll. The only defense against this toxin is to boil the water before drinking as botulism toxin is heat liable and only five minutes of boiling will deactivate it.

3 - 2 Properties Peculiar to BW Agents

Most of the BW agents, particularly the pathogenic microorganisms and toxins, have certain properties not possessed in general by other weapons. They have a delayed action in that a lag or incubation period, often of days, must elapse between the time the victim is exposed to an infectious agent and the time when he comes down with the disease. Identification of microbial agents is difficult and slow as their presence cannot be detected by the unaided senses; it takes hours and usually days for microbial agents to develop in artificial media. However, recently developed immunological procedures such as precipitant, agglutination, immune diffusion, complement fixation, enzyme immune assay (EIA) make for rapid identification of possible BW agents. The microorganisms are living agents in contrast to other agents of warfare. Under favorable conditions pathogenic microorganisms can reproduce and multiply in the host, so that organelle small numbers of pathogens may in time constitute a grave risk to health or perhaps to life. Some contagious pathogens spread from individual to individual and cause epidemics. Most are also quite selective, attacking only certain species of animals or plants. While a given weight of biological agent theoretically may be many times more dangerous than an equal amount of the most effective chemical agent, from a practical stand point its activity is strictly limited by its ability to survive and maintain its virulence under exposure to air, light, cold, dryness and dissemination methods and its ability to overcome the resistance of the target host. Finally, biological agents lend themselves well to covert use, because the small amounts of material needed are easily concealed, transported, and used in sabotage operations. Because of the relatively small amounts required, their cost should be much less than that of other agents of weapons.

3 - 3 Epidemic Spread

A regional outbreak of a contagious disease which attacks many individuals and spreads rapidly is called an epidemic. In each condition there is an fantastic increase in the number of cases of the disease in a limited time among a limited population. In nature, the spread of disease occurs from direct contact between individuals, from contact with or ingestion of excreta and contaminated food, from exposure to dusts and mists of infected material (aerosols), and through transmission by animal or insect vectors. Following large scale dissemination of a biological agent, *an initial outbreak of disease of epidemic proportions might occur*. This might or might not be followed by a secondary or epidemic spread of the disease, depending upon its relative contagiousness, the presence or absence of favorable environmental conditions, and other factors. Since epidemics among the human population can be prevented or controlled by sanitation, immunization, quarantine, and treatment, rapidly spreading epidemics are not considered to be likely aftermath of biological attacks in civilized countries as long as these controlling factors remain at a high level of efficiency. Epizootic among animals have more dangerous possibilities than do epidemics among persons because of the herding and feeding habits of animals; their control or elimination requires extensive use of costly diagnostic and immunological procedures, quarantine where possible, and often the destruction of large numbers of infected animals. Effective measures of preventing or controlling plant epiphytotoics and pest infestations are even more deficient, possibly, because of the tremendous amounts of manpower and materials required, the vectors involved, and the areas to be covered.

3 - 4 Classification
METHODS.

BW agents may be classified subjectively or objectively in several ways, such as kind or type, object of attack, severity of effect produced, viability, virulence, communicability, and tactical or strategic use. Such classifications, for the most part, are not based on hard and fast rules but are relative and often overlapping; they are subject to development of technical knowledge and military doctrine, to such intangible factors as immunity or susceptibility, and to environmental conditions.
TYPE AND KIND OF AGENT.

This classification includes the microorganisms (bacteria, rickettsiae, viruses, protozoa, fungi), the toxins (microbial, zootoxins, and phytotoxins), the pests (of animals, plants, and crops), and the chemical anticrop compounds.
OBJECT OF ATTACK.

Qualitatively, agents can be classified as antipersonnel (man), antianimal (domestic food and draft animals), and anticrop (plants, food, industrial products). There may be some overlapping between antipersonnel and antianimal agents, in that some agents of one group will be effective against members of the other.

SEVERITY.

This may be either lethal or nonlethal. Lethal or killing agents can produce death in susceptible animals or plants, but from a practical standpoint death occurs only in a certain percentage of those exposed. The nonlethal pathogenic agents usually do not kill, but may produce infection or disease with prolonged disability among susceptible, exposed individuals. Food and industrial products may be rendered unfit for use by infestation, injury, or contamination.

VIABILITY.

Viability refers to the ability of BW agents to live and to be infectious after dissemination. The viability of most microorganisms is highly relative. Since BW agents are living organisms, they are significantly affected by environmental conditions. While most vegetative organisms and toxins may be killed or inactivated by several environmental factors, some of the most delicate agents may survive for prolonged periods if conditions are favorable or if natural reservoirs are established. In general, the sporulating bacteria, such as Bacillus anthracis and Clostridium Botulism, and the fungus spores are considered to remain viable for greater periods of time than most of the nonsporulating organisms.

VIRULENCE.

Virulence usually refers to a comparison of the disease producing abilities of different strains of the same agent, those which do not produce disease being termed "avirulent". Virulence depends on a number of factors, such as those having to do with the particular strain of organisms, its passage through living hosts, and the presence or absence of necessary dietary requirements and environmental factors in culture media or host. Strain selection for increased virulence among known organisms is a distinct probability.

COMMUNICABILITY.

A communicable disease is one which is transmitted directly or indirectly from one host to another by contact, body excretions, coughing, or sneezing. Such diseases as diptheria, typhoid fever, mumps, and measles are communicable, while tetanus and botulism are not.

TACTICAL VERSUS STRATEGIC USE.

BW agents, because of their delayed action and for other considerations, would generally be classed as strategic weapons. However, it is possible that in certain situations they might have definite tactical values.

3 - 5 Requisites of Biological Warfare Agents

GENERAL.

Certain requirements are necessary for organisms or substances to be effective biological warfare agents. It is desirable that they possess additional properties which will enhance their value under conditions of use. The selection of a particular biological warfare agent will be governed not only by desired effect but also by the agent's properties and the environmental conditions existing in a given situation. It will usually be impossible for any one agent to fulfill all of these conditions; therefore, in making a selection some compromise may have to be made between optimum and minimum requirements.

BACTERIOLOGICAL WARFARE

REQUIREMENTS.
The agent should meet the following requirements when used against enemy personnel.

- It should consistently produce death, disability, or damage.
- It should be capable of being produced economically and in military adequate quantities from available materials.
- It should be stable under production and storage conditions, in munitions, and in transportation.
- It should be capable of being disseminated efficiently by existing techniques, equipment, or munitions.
- It should be stable after dissemination from military munition.

DESIRABLE CHARACTERISTICS.
The following properties are desirable in agents in certain situations.

- Protection against the agent should be available for the using forces in its preparation, storage, and use.
- It should be difficult for the enemy to detect the agent or to immunize or otherwise protect themselves against it.
- The incubation period should be short and predictable by using forces.
- The persistence of the agent following dissemination should be short and predictable if the contaminated area is to be occupied by friendly troops before the enemy can send in reserves or replacements.
- Under certain conditions, the agent should be capable of producing epidemics.
- It should be capable of attacking or infecting the target by more than one portal of entry and dissemination by various means.
- For tactical use it should produce rapid results.
- It should complement or supplement attack by other weapons.
- It should produce desirable psychological effects.

3 - 6 Comparison With Chemical Warfare Agents
BIOLOGICAL AND CHEMICAL WARFARE AGENTS ARE SIMILAR IN MANY RESPECTS. They are both antipersonnel, rather than antimateriel weapons. They may be dispersed in air and travel with the wind in a similar manner and are capable of contaminating terrain, clothing, equipment, food, and water. Man, animals, and plants are susceptible to attack by these agents in varying degree. Unlike projectiles, they can enter any spot where air can circulate. Variable degrees of protection against both of these agents are afforded by PROTECTIVE MASKS, PROTECTIVE CLOTHING, AND COLLECTIVE PROTECTION DEVICES. Biological agents have advantages over chemical agents in that they can multiply after dispersion under favorable environmental conditions, hence smaller and less costly amounts are needed, and sometimes epidemics might be produced. Biological agents have a DELAYED action of hours or days; some chemical agents act almost immediately and others within a matter of minutes or hours. Field detection of chemical warfare agents is practical. FIELD DETECTION OF BW AGENTS IS NOT POSSIBLE at the present time, as it is necessary to send material to laboratories for preparation of cultures, examination, and identification, a

process which consumes many hours or days. <u>Biological and chemical agents are considered capable of producing similar PSYCHOLOGICAL EFFECTS,</u> especially among personnel not familiar with their properties, limitations, and defensive countermeasures.

3 - 7 Detection and Identification

Detection of a BW agent that has been used in a BW attack is dependent to a great extent upon the observation of unusual circumstances of attack (such as the presence of smokes or mists, strange munitions, or unusual vectors) or upon widespread illness of persons and animals. Periodic examination of specimens caught on a molecular filter (air intake systems) offers a means of detecting and identifying a BW agent under certain conditions and in areas where there is a possibility of a BW attack. The process involved in the identification of a BW agent is difficult even under the most favorable conditions. And in North America, any BW attack will almost certainly be by a terrorist, there will probably be little or no warning. In a BW attack it is probable that unusual disease agents, mixtures of various agents, very high infective doses, and unusual portals of entry or methods of infection will be employed, all of which will make even more difficult the task of identification of the organisms as well as diagnosis of the disease it produces. <u>Diagnosis of the disease produced by recognition of its characteristic symptoms and its reaction to treatment is of value in helping to identify the BW agent, but this can usually be accomplished only days or weeks after the attack or exposure, because of the incubation period required before symptoms are apparent in the host.</u> Samples of probable BW agents are sent to designated laboratories where they are identified by trained technical personnel.

CHAPTER 4

POSSIBLE ANTIPERSONNEL BW AGENTS
3-216/AFM 355-6

4 - 1 General

The Information presented in this section, and else where in this manual on anti personnel agents, is to be found in open scientific literature and therefore is available and, for the most part, known to interested scientific professionals of all countries. It is offered in summarized form to acquaint individuals with the identity and some of the characteristics of certain pathogenic agents that appear to have potential terrorist applications if pertinent existing difficulties can be surmounted.

4 - 2 Objectives

Antipersonnel BW agents are those which are effective directly against man and are selected for their ability to cause death or disability through disease. While these agents might be employed against selected individuals, **their main value would appear to lie in producing epidemics, with their resulting psychological, crippling, or disheartening effects.** The epidemic spread of diseases is most likely when large numbers of infections are produced in dense populations subjected to disaster conditions accompanied by shortages in food, clothing, and shelter.

4 - 3 Targets

Antipersonnel agents might be used against either the military forces or civilian populations, depending on requirements or circumstances, to reduce effective personnel and thus damage production facilities and combat effectiveness. **Areas having large and concentrated populations would furnish the most favorable terrorist targets.** Other objects of attack might be isolated strongholds or fortified islands.

4 - 4 Types

The most promising antipersonnel agents appear to be found among the bacteria and new designer viruses. Bacteria are responsible for many of the serious human diseases and offer a wide variety of choice concerning feasibility of production, stability, viability, portals of entry, casualty-producing effect, transmission, and methods of dissemination. Included among important bacterial diseases of man are staphylococcal food poisoning, scarlet fever, meningococcal meningitis, gonorrhea, diphtheria, tuberculosis, anthrax, tetanus, some pneumonias, blood poisoning, botulism, typhoid and paratyphoid fevers, the bacillary dysenteries, plague, cholera, tularemia brucellosis (undulant fever), glanders, syphilis, yaws, and gas gangrene. The toxins include some of the most poisonous substances known, particularly those produced by the botulism, tetanus, and diphtherial organisms.

CHAPTER 5

Bacteria Likely To Be Used By A Terrorist
TM 3-216/AFM 35-6

The following rating system will be used to denote the probability of these bacteria being selected for use by a terrorist.

- **A= MOST LIKELY EMPLOYED.**
- **B= LESS LIKELY EMPLOYED.**
- **C= LEAST LIKELY EMPLOYED.**

5 - 1 Bacillus Anthracis = A
DESCRIPTION.

B. Anthracis is a rod-shaped, gram-positive, anaerobic sporulating microorganism, the spores constituting the usual infective form. **Anthracis is the most dangerous bacteria that a terrorist could use against North America.** This organism once released will present a problem for decades. An example is the British testing of a anthracis on an island off northern England. After over fifty years the island can not be inhabited. The spores of anthracis can live up to five thousand years. If dispersed over a city, the city may have to be abandoned. Every one who wished to live there would have to be immunized.
DISEASE PRODUCED.

Anthrax may appear in three forms in man- cutaneous, pulmonary, and intestinal. The cutaneous or skin form is also referred to as malignant pustule, occurring most frequently upon the hands and forearms of persons working with infected livestock, and is characterized by carbuncles and swelling at the site of infection. Sometimes this local infection will develop into systemic infection. The pulmonary form, known as wool-sorters disease, is an infection of the lungs contracted by inhalation of the spores; it occurs mainly among workers handling infected hides, wool, and furs. The intestinal form, which is rare in man, is contracted by ingestion of insufficiently cooked meat of infected animals.
SOURCES OF INFECTION.

Cattle, sheep, and horses are the chief animal host, but other animals may be infected. The disease may be contracted by handling of contaminated hair, wool, hides, flesh, blood, and excreta of infected animals, and manufactured products such as bone meal.
MODE OF TRANSMISSION.

Transmission is made through scratches or abrasions of the skin, wounds, inhalation of spores, eating of uncooked infected meat, or by flies.
SUSCEPTIBILITY AND RESISTANCE.

Presumably, all human populations are susceptible. Recovery from an attack of the disease may be followed by immunity.
PREVALENCE.

Anthrax is rare in man and is associated only with animal infections or handling of infected hides and furs.

MORTALITY.

In man, the mortality of untreated cutaneous anthrax ranges up to 25 percent; **in pulmonary cases, it is almost 100 percent, while the intestinal cases usually are fatal.**

IMMUNIZATION.

Artificial active immunization measures have been developed and are available for man (But with terrible side effects). Anti anthracis serum confers some passive immunity.

TREATMENT.

Cutaneous anthrax can be treated effectively with some antibiotics, including **penicillin,** aureomycin, **terramycin,** and chloromycetin, **sulfadiazine;** and immune serum. Similar treatment for respiratory and intestinal infections may be useful in the very early stages, particularly if combined with the use of immune serum, **but is of uncertain value after the disease is well established.**

EPIDEMICITY.

The disease is not epidemic in man. Control of the disease is accomplished by disposal of carcasses (burning or deep burial) and by decontamination of animal products.

STABILITY.

The spores are very stable and may remain alive for many years in soil and water. They will resist sunlight for several days. Steam under pressure or exposure to dry heat above 284 F. for an hour are necessary to kill spores. Effective decontamination also can be accomplished by boiling contaminated articles in water for 30 minutes or by using some of the common disinfectants. Iodine and chlorine are most effective in destroying spores and vegetative cells.

5 - 2 Shigella Dysenteriae = C

DESCRIPTION.

Sh. dysenteriae is a rod-shaped, gram-negative, non motile, non sporulating bacterium.

DISEASE PRODUCED.

Bacillary dysentery, an infectious disease of man, is characterized by mild or severe irritation of the lower gastro intestinal tract; it is usually accompanied by fever, abdominal pain, diarrhea, weakness or prostration, and ulceration of the mucous membranes of the intestine.

SOURCES OF INFECTION.

Feces of infected human patients and carriers are source of infection.

MODE OF TRANSMISSION.

Transmission is made by ingestion of contaminated food, water, or milk; by hand-to-mouth transfer of contaminated material soiled with feces of a patient or carrier; or by flies.

INCUBATION PERIOD.

Incubation is from 1 to 7 days, usually less than 4 days.

SUSCEPTIBILITY AND RESISTANCE.

Most persons are susceptible, but the disease is more common and severe in children than in adults. Recovery from disease is followed by a relative, transitory immunity. Washing, ordinary sterilization methods and use of some of the common disinfectants are effective decontamination measures.

PREVALENCE.

The disease is endemic throughout the world, and epidemics or sporadic outbreaks occur where sanitation is lacking or inadequately applied or enforced, particularly in relation to sewage disposal, food handling and preparation, and infant hygiene. Outbreaks are most common in summer months and occur frequently in large institutions.

MORTALITY.

Mortality is variable, ranging from 2 to 20 percent in untreated cases, depending on the particular strain of organism.

IMMUNIZATION.

At the present time immunization methods for man are satisfactory.

TREATMENT.

Beneficial results may be obtained from treatment with **sulfadiazine, terramycin,** chloromycetin, and aureomycin.

EPIDEMICITY.

The disease is highly contagious, particularly under unsanitary conditions. Control measures include rigid sanitation (careful handling of excreta and adequate sewage disposal) and fly control.

STABILITY.

The dysentery organisms remain viable for considerable periods in water, ice, and mucous discharges but are readily killed by sunlight. Sterilization by steam and common disinfectants are effective decontaminations.

5 - 3 Brucella Group = C

DESCRIPTION.

In this group are included three closely related organisms, Brucella melitensis, Brucella abortus, and Brucella suis. All are nonmotile, nonsporulating, gram-negative, rod-shaped bacilli.

DISEASE PRODUCED.

Brucellosis or undulant fever in man, a general infection, is characterized by irregular prolonged fever, profuse sweating, chills, pain in joints and muscles, and fatigue. The illness last for months, sometimes for years, and may be caused by any one of the three related organisms. Br. Abortis is a parasite of milk cows, producing contagious abortion in cattle; the organism has also been reported in mares, sheep rabbits, and guinea pigs. Br. melitenis is primarily a strict parasite of goats and sheep, Br. suis is a parasite of swine. Br. melitensis and Br. suis are more virulent for man than Br. abortus.

SOURCE OF INFECTION.

Brucella organisms are found in the tissues, milk, and dairy products of infected goats, cattle, and swine.

MODE OF TRANSMISSION.

These diseases are transmitted to man by ingestion of contaminated milk and other dairy products, pickled meats, and uncooked foods and water contaminated by excretions of infected animals; and by direct contact with infected animals or animal products. Infection has also occurred by inhalation and by accidental inoculation among laboratory workers.

INCUBATION PERIOD.

Incubation is from 6 to 60 days or more, averaging 14 days.

SUSCEPTIBILITY AND RESISTANCE.

Most individuals have some degree of resistance or acquired partial immunity to the abortus strains of the organism, probably from ingestion of small doses. Susceptibility of man to BR. melitensis infection ranges from 50 to 80 percent, although it may range from 75 to 80 percent; susceptibility to Br. suis appears to be approximately equal to that of Br. melitensis; susceptibility to BR. abortus appears to be more than 50 percent.

PREVALENCE.

Brucellosis is prevalent in most areas where cattle, goats, and swine are raised. Infection of man occurs more often in males than females, particularly in persons working with cows, hogs, goats, and dairy products, or among those using unpasteurized milk of cows or goats.

MORTALITY.

Mortality of untreated infections is said to average 2 to 3 percent with Br. abortus and 3 to 6 percent with Br. suis and Br. melitensis.

IMMUNIZATION.

Immunization methods are unsatisfactory for man. Immunization of calves is effective as a control measure.

TREATMENT.

The course of the disease may be shortened by appropriate treatment with antibiotics, particularly by a combination of streptomycin and **terramycin.** However, some cases are resistant to all forms of therapy.

EPIDEMICITY.

The disease is not communicable from man to man. Epidemic could result from wide-scale consumption of contaminated, unpasteurized dairy products.

STABILITY.

Brucella organisms will remain alive for weeks in water, unpasteurized dairy products, and soil and are very resistant to low temperatures. Contaminated material are easily sterilized or disinfected by common methods. Pasteurization is effective for contaminated dairy products.

5 - 4 Vibrio Comma = A

DESCRIPTION.

This microorganism is a short, slightly bent, motile gram-negative, non sporulating rod.

DISEASE PRODUCED.

Cholera, an acute infectious gastrointestinal disease of man, is characterized by sudden onset with nausea, vomiting, profuse watery diarrhea with "rice-water" appearance, rapid loss of body fluids, toxemia, and frequent collapse.

SOURCE OF INFECTION.

Feces and vomits of patients, feces of convalescent, and temporary carriers are sources of infection.

MODE OF TRANSMISSION.

Transmission is made through direct or indirect contamination of water or foods, by soiled hands or utensils, or by flies.

INCUBATION PERIOD.

Incubation is from 1 to 5 days, usually 3 days.

SUSCEPTIBILITY AND RESISTANCE.

All populations are susceptible, while natural resistance to infection is variable. Recovery from an attack is followed by a temporary immunity which may furnish some protection for years.

PREVALENCE.

Endemic centers exist in India and southern Asia, from which the disease may spread along human communication lines to more remote countries and cause epidemics. It is normally absent from the Western Hemisphere, however in the last few years it has been appearing with some frequency along the Gulf Coast. Vibro Cholera can live in some shell fish and has been turning up in the southern United States, especially among individuals who eat raw or under cooked shell food.

MORTALITY.

Mortality ranges from about 3 to 30 percent in treated cases to 50 percent in untreated cases.

IMMUNIZATION.

Artificial immunization with vaccines is of variable degree and uncertain duration (6 to 12 months). Acquired immunity last for many years.

TREATMENT.

The first consideration in the treatment of cholera is to replenish fluid and mineral losses of the body. Drug therapy has little or no effect upon the clinical course of the disease. However, chloromycetin, aureomycin, and **terramycin,** given by mouth, causes rapid disappearance of the vibro organisms, thus reducing the spread of the disease.

EPIDEMICITY.

Epidemics is very high under unsanitary conditions, especially those associated with water supplies, foods, and fly control.

STABILITY.

The organism is easily killed by drying. It is not viable in pure water, but will survive up to 24 hours in sewage, and as long as 6 weeks in certain types of relatively impure water containing salts and organic matter. It can withstand freezing for 3 to four days. It is readily killed by dry heat at 212 F., by steam and boiling, by short exposure to ordinary disinfectants, and by chlorination of water.

5 - 5 Corynebacterium Diphtheria = C

DESCRIPTION.

This bacterium (a slender, often slightly curved rod) is gram-positive, non motile, non sporulating, and non acid fast. It varies in size from 2 to 7 microns in length and from 0.5 to 1 micron in diameter. The rodlike forms are usually arranged in palisades and often exhibit club-shaped terminal swellings. They stain irregularly, displaying bars or granules as a result of irregular distribution of protoplasm within the cell. Although the organism is normally aerobic, it is often capable of anaerobic cultivation. It produces a highly potent exotoxin, both in the body and in culture.

DISEASE PRODUCED.

Diphtheria, an acute febrile disease, is generally characterized by local infection, usually involving the air passage. The systemic manifestations are due to absorption of the soluble toxin into the blood stream. The bacteria multiply rapidly in the tonsils, nose, and throat, where grayish membranes patches appear on the mucous membranes, causing sore throat and stoppage of air passages. Skin and wound infections are not uncommon in tropical and subtropical climates. Early diphtheria is usually a surprisingly mild disease unless symptoms of obstruction develop. During the first few days of infection, the throat is not particularly sore, there is only slight fever, and there are no severe constitutional symptoms. This lack of obvious symptoms is characteristic of diphtheria in the adult and is especially dangerous when infection occurs in the nasal passages, because the infection is not recognized or treatment is not begun until sufficient exotoxin has been absorbed to cause irreparable damage to other parts of the body.

SOURCE OF INFECTION.

Discharges from the nose and throat of infected persons and healthy carriers or from skin lesions are sources of infection.

MODE OF TRANSMISSION.

The disease is contracted by direct contact with patients or carriers, by droplet infection, or through articles freshly contaminated with nose and throat discharges of infected individuals.

INCUBATION PERIOD.

The incubation period is usually from 2 to 5 days but occasionally may be longer.

SUSCEPTIBILITY AND RESISTANCE.

Susceptibility is general in the absence of previous contact with the organism or its toxin. In the past there was a very high percentage of immunity in the adult population because of repeated contact with usually unrecognized sources of infection. Because of the current widespread practice of diphtheria vaccination during infancy, there is less frequent opportunity for natural exposure to doses sufficient to produce immunity. Therefore, the adult population is now more susceptible to the disease than in the past. This susceptibility can be accurately measured by means of the Schick test. Recovery from the disease does not necessarily result in immunity.

PREVALENCE.

The disease is endemic and epidemic around the world. it is more common in temperate zones than elsewhere and during the fall and winter. Age distribution of cases and deaths depend largely upon childhood immunization practices.

MORTALITY.

Fatality rate is variable, depending upon the virulence of the infecting strain; among untreated cases it may range from 10 to 50 percent. In cases receiving antitoxin treatment, this rate is lowered to 2 to 8 percent.

IMMUNIZATION.

Diphtheria toxoid is extremely effective. Permanent immunity may be maintained by means of booster inoculations at regular intervals.

TREATMENT.

Diphtheria antitoxin is effective when given promptly and in adequate dosage. **Penicillin** as a supplementary treatment suppresses secondary invaders, shortens the period of illness, and reduces the number of convalescent carriers.

EPIDEMICITY.

Epidemically is high, depending on the immunity status of the population and degree of exposure to the disease. A large proportion of the cases occur in children under 5 years of age.

STABILITY.

The diphtheria organism is more resistant to light, drying, and freezing than are most non- sporulating bacilli, remaining viable for a long time in air and dust. It is capable of surviving many hours on a cotton swab and has been cultured from bits of diphtheritic pseudomembrane after 14 weeks. It is destroyed by ordinary antiseptics and by being boiled for 1 minute or by being heated to 136 F., for 10 minutes.

5 - 6 Bacterium Tularemias (Pasteurella Tularemias) = C

DESCRIPTION.

This is a small, aerobic, gram-negative cocco-bacilli, often varying in size and shape. It is non-motile and non-sporulating.

DISEASE PRODUCED.

Tularemia is also known as rabbit fever and deer fly fever. It is a fatal septicemia (blood poisoning) disease of wild rodents, accidentally communicable to man, in whom it is characterized by sudden onset with chills, fever, and prostration and by a tendency to pneumonia complications. In man it is an acute, severe, weakening disease, later becoming chronic, and may accompanied by enlargement of the regional lymph glands with or without a lesion at the site of infection, or by typhoid like symptoms with no local lesion or enlargement of the local lymph glands.

SOURCE OF INFECTION.

Wild rabbits or hares, deer flies, ticks, and many other animals (including the woodchuck, coyote, opossum, tree squirrel, skunk, cat, deer, fox, hog, sage hen, and some snakes) are sources of infection.

MODE OF TRANSMISSION.

Transmission is made by infection through the skin, eyes, or lungs from handling infected animals, as in skinning or dressing the animals or performing autopsies; by bites of infected flies and ticks; by eating insufficiently cooked rabbit meat; or by drinking contaminated water. Laboratory infections are not infrequent.

INCUBATION PERIOD.

Incubation is from 1 to 10 days, usually about 3 days.

SUSCEPTIBILITY AND RESISTANCE.

All ages are susceptible, and recovery from an attack is followed by permanent immunity. The infectivity rate is from 90 to 100 percent.

PREVALENCE.

The disease is present throughout North America and in many parts of continental Europe and Japan. It occurs in every month of the year in the United States.

MORTALITY.

Untreated cases have a death rate of 4 to 8 percent averaging 5 percent.

IMMUNIZATION.

Vaccination greatly reduces the severity of the disease and may prevent infection in some cases.

TREATMENT.

The antibiotics, particularly streptomycin, aureomycin, and chloromycin, are effective.

EPIDEMICITY.

The disease is essentially sporadic, but may be epidemic when modes of transmission are prevalent. It is not transmitted directly from man to man.

STABILITY.

The organism remains viable for weeks in water, soil, carcasses, and hides, and for years in frozen rabbit meat. It is resistant for months to temperatures of freezing and below. It is rather easily killed by heat at 113F. or above for a few minutes and by only 0.5 percent phenol in 15 minutes.

5 - 7 Yersinia Pestis (Pasteurella Pestis) = A

THIS ORGANISM CAN INFECT BY EITHER THE RESPIRATORY OR ORAL ROUTE, AND CAN BE READILY CULTIVATED IN THE LABORATORY. THIS ORGANISM WOULD ALMOST CERTAINLY BE THE AGENT OF CHOICE, FOR USE BY A TERRORIST.

DESCRIPTION.

Yersinia pestis is a rod-shaped, non-motile, non-sporulating, gram-negative, aerobic bacterium.

DISEASE PRODUCED.

Plague, or black death, occurs as three clinical types in man -- bubonic, pneumonia, and septicemia. Another type of plague, sylvatic plague, is an infectious disease of wild rodent; it is transmissible to man by flea bites. In general, plague is characterized by a rapid clinical course with high fever, extreme weakness, glandular swelling, pneumonia, and/or hemorrhage in the skin and mucous membranes.

Bubonic Plague, the most common, is transmitted to man by the bite of an infected flea, the disease being perpetuated by the rat-flea-rat transmission cycle. The flea bites are usually on the lower extremities where the bacilli spread rapidly through the lymphatic system, enlarging the lymph nodes (buboes) in the groin. The bacilli escape from the nodes, invade the blood stream, and produce a generalized infection. Other parts of the body that are affected are the spleen, lungs, and meninges.

Pneumoniac Plague, **transmitted by inhalation,** spreads rapidly until the entire lung is involved in a hemorrhage , pneumonia process. The disease is usually fatal, the patient dying of suffocation and/or general toxemia.

Septicemia Plague. occurs as the result of gross invasion of the blood stream by plague bacilli, which cause small hemorrhages in the skin and mucous membranes. Death occurs before buboes or pulmonary manifestations appear.

Sylvatic Plague, transmitted by wild rodent fleas, is some what different from plague transmitted by the rat flea (bubonic). The flea bites usually occurring the upper extremities and buboes originate in the armpits rather than in the groin. It frequently changes over to the pneumonia type.

SOURCES OF INFECTION.

Infected rodents and human patients with pneumonia plague are sources of infection. The primary source of the disease is plague of wild rodents, including the ground squirrel, pack rats, and mice of the United States, and various species of wild rodents in other parts of the world. Infection may reach man from these sources or more often through the medium of the domestic rat.

MODE OF TRANSMISSION.

Pneumonia plague is usually transmitted directly from man to man by droplet infection. Bubonic plague is generally transmitted to man by the bites of fleas from infected rats and other rodents.

INCUBATION PERIOD.

Incubation is from 1 to 7 days for pneumonia plague, 4 to 7 days for bubonic plague.

SUSCEPTIBILITY AND RESISTANCE.

Susceptibility is general, particularly to the pneumonia form. Recovery is followed by temporary, relative immunity.

BACTERIOLOGICAL WARFARE

PREVALENCE.

The disease is rare in North America and island possessions of the United States. Occasional cases of the bubonic type occur in the south west from bites of fleas from infected wild rodents. The disease has foci of infection in various parts of the world, particularly in Asia.

MORTALITY.

Untreated bubonic plague has a mortality of 30 to 60 percent, while untreated pneumonia plague kills from 90 to 100 percent of its victims.

IMMUNIZATION.

Antiplague serum produces an artificial passive immunity of 2 week's duration. Active immunization with killed bacterial vaccines is protective for some months when administered 2 or 3 doses at weekly intervals, repeated stimulating doses being necessary. According to some authorities, vaccines prepared from living avirulent strains confer a better and longer immunity than do vaccines from other sources.

TREATMENT.

Prompt treatment with **TETRACYCLINE** and streptomycins combined with serum therapy is essential and is effective if used early. Supportive treatment for pneumonia and septicemia forms is required. These therapies shorten the duration of the disease and reduce its mortality.

EPIDEMICITY.

Bubonic plague is not directly communicable from person to person, but pneumonic plague is intensely communicable during the acute period. Strict area quarantine and sanitation, in addition to other measures such as rat flea extermination, are essential to control outbreaks.

STABILITY.

The organism probably will remain viable in water from 2 to 30 days and in moist meal and grain for about 2 weeks. At near freezing temperatures, it will remain alive from months to years but is killed by 15 minute's exposure to 130F. It also remains viable for some time in dry sputum, flea feces, and buried bodies but is killed by 3 to 5 hours exposure to sunlight. Decontamination if effected by boiling, use of dry heat above 130F. or steam, and treatment with lysol or chloride of lime.

5 - 8 Pseudomonas Mallei (Malleomyces Mallei) = C

DESCRIPTION.

This organism is a slender, non-motile, non-sporulating gram-negative, aerobic, rod-shaped bacterium.

DISEASE PRODUCED.

Glanders, an infection occasionally communicated to man, is characterized by nodular, ulcerative lesions of the skin, mucous membranes, and viscera. It is an acute or chronic disease mainly of horses, mules, and asses, communicable to dogs, goats, and sheep. The acute form is limited to the nasal mucosa and upper respiratory tract; the chronic form, called farcy, is characterized by farcy buds, and pus-forming lesions in the joints and muscles.

SOURCES OF INFECTION.

Infected horses, mules, and asses are sources of infection.

MODE OF TRANSMISSION.

Transmission is usually made by droplet infection (inhalation) or through breaks in the skin; it is sometimes made through the gastrointestinal tract.

INCUBATION PERIOD.

Incubation is from 3 to 5 days.

SUSCEPTIBILITY AND RESISTANCE.

Man is highly susceptible to glanders, and the disease does not confer immunity against a second attack.

PREVALENCE.

Glanders is prevalent among horses, mules, and asses in the Balkans, Russia, Southeastern Asia, and India and is uncommon elsewhere.

MORTALITY.

In untreated cases, the acute form has a mortality of nearly 100 percent, while mortality of the chronic form ranges from 50 to 70 percent.

IMMUNIZATION.

Satisfactory immunization procedures have not been developed.

TREATMENT.

Pseudomonas mallei are notoriously resistant to a large number of commonly used antimicrobial agents; they are usually susceptible to aminoglycosides, the drug of choice.

EPIDEMICITY.

Although the disease is contagious, epidemic spread in man is improbable.

STABILITY.

The organism resists drying for 2 or 3 weeks but is killed by direct sunlight in a few hours. It may remain alive in decaying matter for 2 to 3 weeks. It is easily killed by the common disinfectants and be being heated to 130F. for 10 minutes.

5 - 9 Malleomyces (Pseudomonas) Pseudomallei = C

DESCRIPTION.

This bacterium is motile, non-sporulating, gram- negative, aerobic, rod-shaped, and small (1 to 2 microns long and 0.5 microns wide) It is often marked be bipolar staining. It closely resembles Pseudomonas mallei.

DISEASE PRODUCED.

Malioidosis, also known as Whitmore's disease, is a glanders like disease primarily of rodents but occasionally found in man. It tends to run a more rapid course than glanders does and in man is almost always acute and rapidly fatal, death occurring usually in 3 to 4 weeks, Recently, reports of chronic infections involving lungs and lymph glands, bones, joints, and legs have appeared. The disease is characterized by sudden onset with severe chills, high fever, rapid prostration, headache, muscle and joint pains, cough, labored breathing, nausea, and vomiting. In a short time, numerous small abscesses form in the skin, bones, lymph nodes, lungs, and other internal organs.

SOURCE OF INFECTION.

Probable sources of infection are food or other materials contaminated with rodent excreta and possibly by rat fleas.

MODE OF TRANSMISSION.

Transmission takes place apparently by ingestion of food contaminated with excreta of infected rats and by rat flea bites.

INCUBATION PERIOD.

Although not accurately known, the incubation period is from a few days to years.

SUSCEPTIBILITY AND RESISTANCE.

Susceptibility is general but the organism apparently is not extremely infectious under natural conditions, considering the low prevalence of human disease in endemic areas. However, man appears to have little or no resistance to it once infection is established.

PREVALENCE.

Cases of the disease have been found chiefly in the Malay States, Indochina, and Ceylon. They have also been reported in Guam and the Philippine Islands and recently in the united states.

MORTALITY.

Acute melioidoses is usually fatal.

IMMUNIZATION.

No vaccine have been developed. Little is known of any immunity acquired through infection.

TREATMENT.

Pseudomonas pseudomallei are notoriously resistant to a large number of commonly used antimicrobial agents; they are usually susceptible to aminoglycosides, the drug of choice.

EPIDEMICITY.

The disease is normally not contagious. Spread by droplet infection might occur in a cold climate, which is more suitable to this type of transmission.

STABILITY.

The organism is extremely resistant to drying and may survive a month or more in dried soil, in excreta, and in water. It is easily killed in 10 minutes by 1.0 percent phenol or 0.5 percent formalin and by moist heat at 133F.

5 - 10 Salmonella Typhosa (Typhia) = A

DESCRIPTION.

This organism is a rod-shaped, motile, non-sporulating, gram-negative bacterium. It is also known as S. typhi.

DISEASE PRODUCED.

Typhoid fever is a systemic infection characterized by continued fever, lymphoid tissue involvement, ulceration of the intestines, enlargement of the spleen, rose-colored spots on the skin, diarrhea, and constitutional disturbances.

SOURCES OF INFECTION.

Feces and urine of infected individuals and carriers are sources of infection.

MODE OF TRANSMISSION.

Transfer of organisms is made through the alimentary tract by direct contact with a typhoid patient or a chronic carrier; by consumption of contaminated water, food, milk, or shellfish; and by flies.

INCUBATION PERIOD.

Incubation is from 3 to 38 days, usually 7 to 14 days.

SUSCEPTIBILITY AND RESISTANCE.

Susceptibility is general, except that some adults have an acquired immunity from unrecognized infection. Recovery usually is followed by permanent immunity.

PREVALENCE.

The disease is widespread throughout the world. Once endemic and epidemic in most large cities of North America, it has been steadily falling in incidence, particularly in areas supplied with safe water and pasteurized milk, and where modern sewage disposal facilities are used. It is still endemic in some rural areas of the United States, usually as sporadic cases or in small carrier or contact epidemics.

MORTALITY.

The mortality in untreated cases range from 0 to 10 percent.

IMMUNIZATION.

Inoculation with typhoid vaccine produces an artificial active immunity of about 2 years' duration. High protection lasting for about a year can be maintained by annual booster injections of vaccine.

TREATMENT.

Prompt use of appropriate antibiotics chloromycetin, aureomycin, tetracycline shortens the period of communicability and rapidly cures the disease.

EPIDEMICITY.

Epidemicity is high in the presence of carriers; in the absence of sanitary control for water, food, and milk supplies; and where individuals are not protected by immunization.

STABILITY.

The organism remains viable for 2 to 3 weeks in water, up to 3 months in ice and snow, and for 1 to 2 months in fecal material. Pasteurization, exposure to 132F. for 20 minutes, exposure to 5 percent phenol or 1:500 bichloride of mercury for 5 minutes, cooking, and boiling are effective decontamination measures.

5 - 11 Salmonella Paratyphi And Salmonella Schottmuelleri = C.

DESCRIPTION.

These organisms are short, plump, rod-shaped, motile, non-sporulating, gram-negative bacteria. S. paratyphi is known at type A of the group; S. schottmuelleri is known as S, paratyphi B.

DISEASE PRODUCED.

Paratyphoid fever (an acute, febrile, generalized infection) is very similar to typhoid fever (indistinguishable clinically), but its symptoms are usually milder. It is characterized by continued fever severe diarrhea, and abdominal pain, with involvement of the lymphoid tissues of the intestines, enlargement of the spleen, and sometimes rose-colored spots on the trunk. S schottmuelleri (type B) is responsible for more cases of the disease than type A and may also produce gastroenteritis. (salmonella hirschfeldii (S. paratyphoid C) may also produce paratyphoid fever.

SOURCES OF INFECTION.

Contaminated feces and urine of patients and carriers are sources of infection.

MODE OF TRANSMISSION.

Transfer of organisms is the same as for typhoid.

INCUBATION PERIOD.

Incubation is variable, from 1 to 10 days, depending on strain of organism but averaging less than a week.

SUSCEPTIBILITY AND RESISTANCE.

Susceptibility is general, and recovery is followed by permanent immunity.

PREVALENCE.

The disease is world-wide, but incidence has declined with that of typhoid. Outbreaks are sporadic or limited and are due to contact or to consumption of contaminated foods such as milk or water. There are probably many unrecognized cases. Paratyphoid fever caused by S. hirschfeldii has been found relatively frequent in parts of Asia, Africa, and southeast Europe but is almost unknown in the United States.

MORTALITY.

Fatalities are low, perhaps between 1 and 2 percent.

IMMUNIZATION.

Paratyphoid vaccine for types A and B is usually incorporated with typhoid vaccine.

TREATMENT.

Chemotherapy with "sulfa" drugs and use of antibiotics, such as chloromycetin, aureomycin, streptomycin, tetracycline, shorten the period of communicability and hasten cure of the disease.

EPIDEMICITY.

The epidemicity is similar to that for typhoid, depending on presence of carriers; inadequate sanitary controls for water, food, and mild supplies; and absence of immunization.

STABILITY.

Stability is the same as for S. typhosa. Decontamination measures include chlorination, pasteurization, boiling, and cooking.

5 - 12 Salmonella Typhimurium = C.

DESCRIPTION.

This bacterium is a short plump rod which occurs singly and measures 0.5 micron in width and from 1 to 1.5 microns in length. It is gram-negative, non-sporulating, and motile.

DISEASE PRODUCED.

Salmonella food poisoning (gastroenteritis) is most frequently caused by S. typhimurium in man. The onset of the infection is nearly always sudden, characterized by headache, chills, and usually abdominal pains. This is followed by nausea, vomiting, and severe diarrhea with a rise in temperature and prostration. Recovery is usually complete within 2 to 4 days.

SOURCE OF INFECTION.

The source of infection are usually rodents, especially rats and mice, and human carriers who handle food, eggs, and meat from diseased animals.

MODE OF TRANSMISSION.

The disease is usually obtained by the ingestion of contaminated food (particularly meat), water, or milk. It may also be obtained by direct contact with infected persons or carriers, by direct contact with articles contaminated by discharges (feces, urine, and vomits) of infected persons or carriers, or from flies.

INCUBATION PERIOD.

Food poisoning occurs usually after an incubation period ranging from 6 to 24 hours but seldom after more than 48 hours. The short interval suggests that large numbers of the organism are usually ingested.

SUSCEPTIBILITY AND RESISTANCE.

Susceptibility is general. The disease is more severe infants and young children than in adults. Natural immunity is believed to exist in some persons, while acquired immunity is usually permanent after recovery from the disease. The bacterium is primarily pathogenic for animals; in mice it produces a typhoid like disease with high mortality.

PREVALENCE.

The disease is widely distributed geographically and occurs in almost all warm blooded animals.

MORTALITY.

Fatalities range from 1 to 2 percent in epidemics.

IMMUNIZATION.

Vaccination is not practical.

TREATMENT.

Treatment is mainly physiological. A saline purge is indicated if the infected food has not been eliminated by nature. The restoration of fluid balance is most important, particularly in the very young and old. Streptomycin, chloromycetin, terramycin, tetracycline, and aureomycin reduce the number of organisms in the intestinal tract.

EPIDEMICITY.

The infection is contagious. Epidemics usually occur when mass consumption of contaminated food occurs. Explosive epidemics occur in animals, particularly rodents, and many surviving animals become chronic carriers. Spread of the infection can be halted by elimination of carriers as food handlers, proper sanitation, pasteurization of milk, elimination of rodents and flies where food is prepared, and careful handling adequate cooking of food.

STABILITY.

Stability of this organism is typical of the group.

5 - 13 **Mycobacterium Tuberculosis = C.**

DESCRIPTION.

Tubercle bacilli are slender straight or slightly curved rods with rounded ends. They vary from 0.2 to 0.5 micron in width and from 1 to 4 microns in length. They are acid-fast, non-motile, and gram-positive and are strictly aerobic.

DISEASE PRODUCED.

Pulmonary tuberculosis is characterized by severe lung involvement accompanied by cough, fever, fatigue, and loss of weight. This form of the disease is the chief cause of morbidity and mortality. The primary type is acute, healing or progressive in a relatively short time, and is most commonly seen in infants and children and occasionally in adults who have escaped childhood infection. Adults acquiring their first infection may manifest the post-primary type, passing through the primary phase inconspicuously because of its rapid development. The post-primary (reinfection) type is more stable and more chronic than the primary type and is associated with a significant, but inadequate, degree of resistance. Tuberculosis infection in the bones, joints, skin, or other tissues is usually caused by the bovine variety of M. tuberculosis, although this type may also invade the lung.

SOURCE OF INFECTION.

Infection is acquired from persons with draining lung cavities. Tuberculous cattle, particularly their raw milk, is the source of the bovine variety, which is rare in the United States until recently, now several states have reported that tuberculoses is being detected in deer herds, which can quickly spread into dairy cattle. For the first time since 1953, the United States experienced a 1.1% increase in new active cases of tuberculosis in 1986; it is thought that this increase is related to the acquired immune deficiency syndrome (AIDS) epidemic. A remarkable increase in infection due to M. avium complex can also be attributed to AIDS patients.

MODE OF TRANSMISSION.

Transmission usually occurs through the discharges of the respiratory tract, by direct or indirect personal contact. In the United States, primary infection is almost always a result of inhalation of the bacilli in droplet form. The post-primary type of tuberculosis may be caused either by organisms which have survived in primary lesions or by newly inhaled bacilli. The bovine type is acquired by contact with tuberculous cattle or ingestion of their raw milk but can be transmitted also by the same route as the human type, from person to person. Natural infection usually requires continued and intimate exposure.

SUSCEPTIBILITY AND RESISTANCE.

Man is very susceptible to tuberculoses infection but remarkably resistant to tuberculous disease. Susceptibility to the disease is dependent upon age, **race,** family characteristics, and previous exposure to the organism. It is lowest in persons from 3 to 12 years of age and is greater in the undernourished and fatigued and among people who have not previously been exposed to the disease. **In the United States the rapidly progressive primary type is seen more often in young adult Negroes than in white adults.** Recovery from the disease leaves no solid immunity, but resistance is altered so that reinfection is not as acute as the previous infection. The chance of contracting progressive clinical tuberculosis is higher in tuberculin negative than in tuberculin-positive individuals.

PREVALENCE.

Tuberculosis is one of the most common of the infectious diseases of man. It occurs in all parts of the world, although it has never appeared in some isolated groups of people. In the third world countries, infection is widespread in the urban population, as is shown by the 50 to 95 percent tuberculin reactor rate, but the progressive disease develops only in a small proportion of those infected.

MORTALITY.

Fatality rate is high especially among infants, adult males up to old age, and adolescent and young adult females. Despite the many improvements in case-finding and the newer therapeutic procedures, there now is appearing a drug resistant strain of tuberculosis in whole or part resulting from the AIDS patients. This new strain is a fast growing killer strain, and in the future tuberculosis could return to being among the ten leading causes of death in the United States.

IMMUNIZATION.

Vaccination of tuberculin-negative persons with living strains of attenuated tubercle bacilli of Calmette and Guerin confers some protection against naturally acquired tuberculous disease (primary and postprimary). However, prevention and control of tuberculosis depends largely upon detection and isolation of carriers and the general improvement of environmental and economic conditions.

TREATMENT.

Streptomycin, particularly when combined with paraaminosalicylic acid (PSA) or isonicotinic acid hydrazide (INH), is valuable in arresting the disease, particularly in its acute manifestations, but this treatment in itself is not curative. Success in treatment depends upon supportive therapy, including rest, good food (supplementing the diet with vitamins A, C, and D), and fresh air. Local rest of the lungs is promoted by several methods. Surgery is required in some cases. However, with the new drug resistant strains coming from the AIDS patients, the only treatment is prevention.

EPIDEMICITY.

The spread of tuberculosis occurs in large part through continued family or household case association, the disease being transmitted slowly from one generation to the next. Under favorable conditions, epidemic outbreaks may take place. Occurrence is influenced by occupation, as by continued exposure to mineral (silica) dust, which predisposes to infection.

STABILITY.

When organisms are exposed to direct sunlight, in artificial culture they are killed in 2 hours, but sputum under the same conditions they may survive 20 to 30 hours. When organisms are protected from the sun, they will live in putrefying sputum for weeks and in dried sputum for as long as 6 to 8 months. They are resistant to the usual chemical disinfectants, 24 hours being required for the decontamination of sputum by 5 percent phenol, but possess no greater resistance to moist heat than other bacteria do, being killed in 15 to 20 minutes at 140F. Pasteurization is effective in destroying the organisms in milk.

CHAPTER 6

BIOTOXINS
TM 3-216/AFM 355-6

6 - 1 Botulism Toxin

DESCRIPTION.

This is the protein-like exotoxin formed by the botulism bacillus. Through repeated purification procedures it has been obtained in a crystalline form and is the most powerful poison known. The crude material or "mud" is a brownish, amorphous mass. There are at least five distinct types, A, B, C, D, and E, of which types A, B, and E are known to be toxic for man; C and D are toxic for animals and probably for man.

DISEASE PRODUCTION.

Botulism is a highly fatal, acute poisoning. It is characterized by vomiting, constipation, thirst, general weakness, headache, fever, dizziness, double vision, dilation of the pupils, paralysis of muscles of swallowing, and difficulty of speech. Respiratory paralysis is the usual cause of death.

SOURCE OF THE TOXIN.

Sources of the toxin are the bacteria Clostridium botulinum and Cl. para-botulinum, which are rod-shaped, slightly motile, sporulating, gram-positive, anaerobic bacilli. The principal reservoir of the bacteria is soil. The bacteria grow and form their toxin under anaerobic conditions, usually in improperly canned, non-acid foods such as meats; and some vegetables, including corn, string beans, spinach, and olives.

MODE OF TRANSMISSION.

Transmission is through eating of food contaminated with botulinum toxin. The bacteria do not grow or reproduce in the human body, poisoning is due entirely to the toxin already formed in the ingested material. Fresh foods are not involved; freshly well-cooked foods are not involved, as heating destroys the toxin. Possibly the toxin could be introduced through breaks in the skin or by inhalation.

LATENT PERIOD.

Symptoms of poisoning usually do not appear until 12 to 72 hours after food containing the toxin has been ingested. The length of time depends upon the amount of toxin contained in the food.

SUSCEPTIBILITY AND RESISTANCE.

All persons are susceptible to poisoning. The few who recover from the disease have an active immunity of uncertain duration and degree.

PREVALENCE.

The disease has world-wide distribution. It is prevalent wherever improperly canned food products are consumed.

MORTALITY.

Mortality is approximately 65 percent in the United States but is low in Europe; it is directly related to the amount of toxin consumed.

IMMUNIZATION.

Passive immunization with antitoxin appears to be encouraging as a protective measure for humans but is of little therapeutic value. Active immunization with botulinum toxoid is of proved protective value.

TREATMENT.

Treatment is mainly supportive. Antitoxin therapy is of doubtful value, particularly where large doses of the poison have been consumed.

EPIDEMICITY.

The disease is not contagious. Epidemics occur only where widespread distribution and consumption of a contaminated food product have occurred.

STABILITY.

The toxin is stable for a week in non-moving water where it is not aerated. It persists for a long time in food when it is not exposed to air. The toxin is destroyed when boiled for 15 minutes, but botulinum spores resist boiling for 6 hours. Pressure cooking will destroy spores. Botulinum toxin differs from other bacterial toxins in that it is not destroyed by gastrointestinal secretions.

6 - 2 Staphylococcus Toxin.

DESCRIPTION.

The toxin is produced in food by certain strains of staphylococci. It is an entero-toxin, as it has a specific action on the cells of the intestinal mucosa. Unlike most bacterial exotoxin, it is stable at boiling temperature and antigenically is irregular in eliciting the formation of immune bodies.

DISEASE PRODUCED.

A food poisoning (not infection) is produced following the ingestion of food in which various strains of staphylococci have been growing. It is usually characterized by sudden, sometimes violent, onset, with severe nausea, vomiting, stomach cramps, severe diarrhea, and prostration. Patients usually feel normal 24 hours after the attack begins.

SOURCE OF POISONING.

The source of contamination is not known in most cases but is probably of human origin. Food implicated as sources of food poisoning are chiefly (creamy), milk (raw) and milk products, and meat. Food handlers who are nasal or skin carriers of pathogenic staphylococci or who have an open staphylococcal lesion on hands, arms, or face have been traced as sources of poisoning. The implicated foods usually are allowed to remain at a warm temperature before consumption, thus providing an incubation period for formation of toxin.

MODE OF TRANSMISSION.

Consumption of contaminated custard filled pastry; processed meats, particularly ham; and perhaps milk from cows with infected udders are modes of transmission. Improper food handling is responsible for many outbreaks.

LATENT PERIOD.

Incubation is relatively short. One-half hour to 4 hours, usually 2 to 4 hours, elapse between ingestion of food and appearance of symptoms.

SUSCEPTIBILITY AND RESISTANCE.

Most persons are susceptible, but individual reactions are variable.

PREVALENCE.

The toxin is world-wide and is probably the principal cause of acute "food poisoning".

MORTALITY.

Fatalities are rare.

IMMUNIZATION.

There is no immunization.

TREATMENT.

Treatment is supportive.

EPIDEMICITY.

Food poisoning is non-contagious. Most outbreaks are small and are confined to persons who have eaten the same contaminated food.

STABILITY.

The toxin is resistant to freezing, to boiling for 30 minutes, and to potable concentrations of chlorine. The organisms remain viable after 67 days of refrigeration.

BACTERIOLOGICAL WARFARE

CHAPTER 7

DISSEMINATION
TM 3-216/AFM 355-6

7 - 1 General Considerations.

    The term "dissemination" as used in this text refers to various procedures that might be developed and applied in launching BW attacks against man. Selection of munitions, devices, and methods is governed by the type and characteristics of the agent, the object of attack, the results to be achieved, and environmental and meteorological conditions. There are many obvious ways in which BW attacks can be attempted. They may include methods previously used for other kinds of warfare and new or conjectural procedures that have not been considered. **Peculiar characteristics of biological agents which favor them in comparison with other types of agents are the relatively minute amounts required, since they are living and can multiply in the victim. Other characteristics are; difficulty of detection or recognition; slowness of identification; delayed action; spread or epidemic potential; and suitability for subversive or sabotage use.** These properties are valuable assets in that they make a wide range of dissemination methods possible. Citizens should be familiar with probable ways of dissemination, principles of biological attack, properties of biological attack, and properties of biological agents, so that they can promptly recognize and report a BW attack to whom ever can spread the word the quickest. A BW attack should be anticipated whenever the United Nations and their collaborators are hell-bent on forcing a little country, which has strayed out of line, back into line. Perhaps that country has a few dozen agents equipped with BW weapons already in place in the United States, ready to act if Washington tries something. Small countries are more likely to employ BW than more powerful countries. Limited resources also encourages novel and unusual methods of dissemination, especially those adopted for aerosol dissemination or generation. <u>The procedure logical for an individual agent or agents</u> is the use of free balloons. The device could be small, equipped with an altimeter release, and weigh only a few kilograms with the attaching ring for the balloon (a surplus weather balloon would be probable). A small cylinder of helium or a hydrogen gas generator would inflate the balloon. The procedure that the agent would most likely follow, would be to select a city, town, or strategic target, call the weather bureau or flight service station for the winds aloft, temperature, and barometric pressure. He would then decide if he desired a day or night attack, (a night attack could result in more casualties, owing that the bacteria would live longer by not being exposed to sunlight), or waiting for an overcast day. Get up wind, determine the rate of rise for the balloon, wind speed, distance to target, (these charts are readily available from the weather bureau for use with weather balloons), and set the altimeter release. The sight of a weather balloon is not very uncommon and would raise few suspicions. Once the balloon got to the altitude for release, as determined by the altimeter, and released its load, the balloon would have a much lighter load and quickly gain altitude. Normally weather balloons travel up to approximately 30 thousand feet and burst, and the instrument package is returned to earth by a simple parachute. Each year the vast majority of these instrument packages are never returned to the weather bureau, even though they have marked on the outside container clear instructions for the instrument package to be turned in at the nearest post office to be returned to the weather bureau. Unfortunately, the same would probably hold true for the balloon bacterial dissemination device. If the device were to be used along the North American east coast, with the balloon bursting out over the Atlantic ocean, recovery and possible tracking to the agency responsible for the attack would be more difficult. Parachutes or other devices for bacterial dissemination, could be used from small single engine aircraft. Flasks or ampoules or any type of weapons that produce no apparent or immediate effect could also be used. North American citizens should also be alert to detect and guard against attempts at sabotage, the possibilities of which are of great variety. Unusual flights or objects should be noted and reported.

7.2 **Special Considerations.**

Special considerations, not applicable to other forms of warfare, should be understood when an attempt is made to provide defense against BW attack. These considerations apply to measures that might be used to surprise, confuse, or overwhelm enemy forces and are concerned with the nature of the agents used, the methods of their employment, and vulnerability of the target. Undoubtedly efforts will be directed toward increasing the virulence of the biological agent to the highest degree possible. Continual attempts will be made to produce strains of organisms that have more than ordinary resistance to antibiotic, chemotherapeutic, and other treatment methods. If possible, newly isolated disease producing organisms or ones not ordinarily present in the target population will probably be given serious consideration. Various combinations of similar or dissimilar agents might be employed simultaneously to hinder identification and produce more than one disease in the same individual, thus confusing diagnosis by presenting different or contradictory symptoms or periods of incubation. Attempts might also be made to use combinations of BW agents that help to make the other more effective (synergistic effect). It might also be possible, by using biological and chemical agents at the same time or in close succession, to produce infections from the BW agent more easily in individuals injured by the chemical agent. **In general, attempts most probably would be directed toward much higher exposure concentration of an agent than occur under normal conditions to overcome natural or artificial defenses.** Efforts would probably be made to effect entrance of agents through portals of entry not normally used in naturally occurring infections. Such an entrance might be accomplished through adjustment of the particle size of agents dispersed as mist or dusts. For instance, the natural method of infection in plague is through anthropoid bites and in tularemia is usually through breaks in the skin. **However, if any of these agents -- Plague, Cholera, Typhoid fever, or Anthrax were inhaled in sufficiently small particles, infection might be established by inoculation through the lungs. Inhalation of larger particles which are not small enough to enter the alveolar, or small air passages of the lungs, would result in trapping some of these particles in the upper air passages. From there they would be wafted by cilia to the mouth and pharynx; those which were not then expectorated would be swallowed. Infection might be established through the gastrointestinal tract by agents that produce such diseases as plague and tularemia.** It is also probable that insect vectors, such as flies, could be used to transmit agents of disease other than those which they have been known to carry. Reducing populations of insects such as flies would help reduce the spread of infection.

7 - 3 Physical States Of Agent Munitions.

   Since most microorganisms are living particulate substances, there are only two possible physical states in which they can be disseminated, that is, solid forms or liquid suspensions. Solid forms consist of dense aggregates of material, or finely divided powders or dusts, but only the powders or dusts would be effective for dissemination over wide areas in the form of clouds or aerosols. It might be possible to produce and store in dry form some pathogenic vegetative organisms or spores, which would remain virulent for long periods of time. It is probable that methods could be developed to project these spores effectively against an enemy either in cloud attacks, in missiles of various kinds, or by **covert or hidden methods.** Liquid suspensions of organisms or spores can be disseminated as mist by **suitable spraying devices, generators, and explosive projectiles (as has been done with chemical agents), or clandestinely in small bottles or other containers. In aerosol attacks against man, when a toxic agent is used which has to enter the lungs to establish an infection, effective penetration occurs only if the sizes of the aerosol particles are within certain narrow limits.**

7 - 4 Overt And Covert Attack.

   Attack with BW agents may be classified either as overt (open) or as covert (hidden). Overt attack implies the adaptation and use of principles and methods of attack and use of weapons and munitions previously developed, known, and commonly accepted in warfare. Covert attack refers to the stealthy employment either of accepted methods or of unusual or sabotage methods that might be used before or after the actual outbreak of hostilities. While there is no direct evidence that effective methods for disseminating BW agents have been developed, there are numerous possibilities, obvious or theoretical, which deserve consideration. Both overt and covert attacks are possible from the air, from the ground, and from the sea.

7 - 5 Airborne Methods.

Airplanes and, to a lesser extent, *balloons* can be used to disseminate BW agents by various techniques against enemy personnel, installations, and cities. It is probable that *spray tanks* and clusters of bombs could be adapted to launch cloud attacks of BW mists or dusts from the air against man and that generating devices could be dropped which would automatically function in a similar manner upon reaching the ground or surface of the sea. **It would be theoretically possible to launch a covert BW attack from great distances against enemy countries by using high altitude prevailing winds to deliver infectious agents by means of balloons or other buoyant devices.** Rockets or guided missiles containing epidemic agents could be directed against areas where personnel were highly concentrated, and contaminated food materials could be dropped in city slum regions to set up foci of infection among sewer rats. It would also be possible to release infected animal vectors of disease in containers or crates equipped with parachutes and automatic opening devices.

7 - 6 Ground Methods.

   Under favorable meteorological conditions, cloud attacks in the form of mists or dusts could be projected by generators against enemy personnel. These devices could be installed at fixed intervals on a stationary front or operated from vehicles moving parallel to the front. In such operations favorable winds would be required, and it would be desirable that friendly troops were protected against the agent either by protective devices or by immunization, especially if movement into the contaminated area was imminent. BW attack could be launched deep into enemy occupied areas by shell with low-bursting charges or by rockets and guided missiles equipped with BW warheads. It even might be practical to construct small arms projectiles containing BW agents that could produce infections even in single wounds. In withdrawal actions, disengaged areas could be sown with BW mines, or surfaces and structures could be contaminated by other methods.

7 - 7 Seaborne Methods.

Cloud attack with BW mists or dusts can be launched in the presence of favoring inshore winds, preferably at night, against enemy coastal cities or troop concentrations by means of generating or spraying devices installed on surface or undersea craft. Daylight attacks from surface craft probably would not be detectable, even if suspected by the enemy, and night attacks could not be recognized. Floating mines equipped with generating devices could either be placed by surface or undersea craft or dropped by aircraft and set to operate at a predetermined time against coastal targets. Rockets, guided missiles, and shell containing BW agents could be delivered against coastal areas and island strongholds.

7 - 8 Sabotage Possibilities.

Sabotage refers to concealed or insidious action by enemy agents or sympathizers to interfere with or obstruct the defense effort of a nation. **Biological warfare would appear to lend itself particularly well to such covert or undercover operations because of detection difficulties, the variety of agents and the way in which they might be used, and the small amounts of materials required.** It would be quite possible for a potential enemy nation to initiate sabotage with biological agents before, as well as after, a declaration of war, and such attempts might be quite effective even though the attacked nation subsequently became aware of them. The object of such covert attacks would be to kill or injure man and animals, to deplete the food supply, and to reduce a nation's capacity to defend itself or wage war by lowering morale.

Large-scale covert attacks might be attempted by utilization of prevailing winds or high altitude air masses to carry infective material or devices from areas far distant from the country that was the object of attack. **Small-scale sabotage attacks rather than large-scale attacks would appear to be more practical, because they would be directed against small segments of the human population or perhaps against key individuals. <u>In these operations, agents or sympathizers would be secretly furnished infective material, or they would produce or obtain it themselves, that they could disseminate stealthily by various methods. Small dusting or spraying devices could be used to introduce agent material into the ventilating systems of large office buildings, auditoriums, and theaters with little danger of detection.</u>** Infective microbes and toxins could be pumped directly into the mains of city water supply or introduced by use of back-siphoning principles that might be applied even in private homes. Agents working in pharmaceutical establishments could contaminate medicinal products. Various methods could be used to contaminate unprocessed and uncooked foods, and infective material could be placed in cooked or processed foods, such as milk, by food handlers and servers. Effective measures might also be developed to distribute pathogens on currency, stamps, and in cosmetics, shaving soap, chewing gum, and other articles.

CHAPTER 8

BIOLOGICAL WARFARE
FM 21-41

8 - 1 You Must Know The Score.

    This book is for you, the North American Citizen. Its purpose is to help you perform your job under BW conditions and live to tell about it. The material presented in this manual is applicable to both germ and biotoxin warfare.

    When any poison gets into your body, it can cause sickness or death. Likewise, when biotoxin, or biological attacks occur, some casualties are certain. Casualties are citizens put out of action -- sick, wounded, missing, or killed. Biological agents cause casualties just as bullets and high explosives do. Whether you are a casualty will depend on your knowledge. Learn now what you can do to protect yourself and to help maintain the effectiveness of your community. The skill of you, the individual North American Citizen, in protecting yourself will help determine the success of your community.

    Users of this book are encouraged to submit recommended changes or comments for its improvement. Comments should be keyed to the specific page, paragraph, and line of the text in which change is recommended. Reasons should be provided for each comment to insure understanding and complete evaluation. Comments should be forwarded direct to my attention.

8 - 2 Why This Book Was Written

    By studying this book you will learn basic facts that you must know in order to survive biological attacks and maintain your community.

8 - 3 How To Get The Most From This Book

    As you read and study this book, ask yourself the following questions:
- a. What are Biological operations ?
- b. How can biological agents injury or kill me?
- c. How may I be attacked?
- e. How can I protect myself against biological agents?
- f. What can I do to help in minimizing the number of casualties in my community?

In this book are the facts which answer these questions for you. Remember them! They can save your life!

8 - 4 Why Biological Warfare Must Be Taken Seriously
GENERAL.

    The purpose of biological warfare is to produce casualties in man and animals and to cause damage to plants and material.
BIOLOGICAL OPERATIONS.

    The effects of harmful microorganisms (germs) are well known to you. You have probably experienced the effects of disease such as colds, dysentery, measles, mumps, and chickenpox. Such diseases are caused by certain types of harmful microorganisms which get into your body and multiply, thus producing infection. Microorganisms are living organisms that are so small they can be seen only through a microscope. Of the thousands of them in the world around us, the vast majority are harmless or actually beneficial to man. Only a few of the disease-producing microorganisms are harmful enough to be considered for employment as biological agents. A biological operation is the employment of biological agents by a weapon system to produce casualties or damage. A group of larger organisms, capable of carrying a disease-producing microorganism to an individual or from one individual to another, are known as vectors and also can be considered for use in biological operations. These vectors include, but are not limited to, flies, misquotes, fleas, ticks, and lice.

8 - 5 How The Enemy May Attack You

The following are examples of munitions and methods that a modern enemy may use against you in biological warfare. These are regarded as sound methods of conducting operations. However, other means of attack are possible and may be used by an enemy to achieve surprise.

- ◆ 1. SABOTAGE.
- ◆ 2. FREE BALLOONS.
- ◆ 3. GENERATORS.
- ◆ 4. AIRPLANE SPRAY.
- ◆ 5. VECTORS.

Incapacitating or fatal diseases can result when biological agents are inhaled, reach the stomach through consumption of contaminated food or water, or are introduced through the skin. Protecting yourself so that you can continue your job against an enemy (foreign or domestic) using biological agents is your primary concern. To protect yourself against any danger, you must know what the danger is, how it affects you, and how to recognize its presence. Correct individual defensive measures can protect you from many of the hazards you may face from biological agents. Learning these measures can mean not only that you live to tell about it, but also that your community stays on the job to defeat the enemy.

FIGURE 8.1

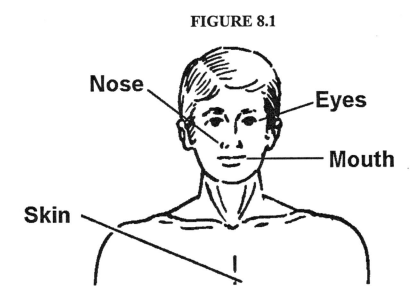

8 - 6 Where Toxic Agents Attack, Where Toxic Agents Can Enter Your Body

After looking at figure 8.1, you may rightly conclude that any equipment that will keep biological agents out of your lungs, out of your eyes, and off your skin will **PROTECT** you. The types of protective equipment provided and the protective measures needed to block the entry of biological agents into your body are described in the chapters which follow. As a well-trained citizen of North America, you must know how to use your protective equipment, and how to make the most of any shelter you may have. Using this knowledge, you will be prepared to protect yourself against the weapons of Germ warfare and, at the same time, to carry on your job.

An important consideration in protecting yourself and continuing your job in any future conflict is to realize that the danger of chemical and biological operations may exist simultaneously or separately. The enemy will use any weapon or any combination of weapons that he thinks will put you and your community out of action. This means that he may use chemical weapons and then follow up with a biological attack. He may use toxic chemical weapons to contaminate certain areas in the hope of making our citizens more vulnerable to biological attack. He may use biological agents to inflict personnel losses, hoping to lower your community's defensive power against his assaults. Learn now how to protect yourself against all the weapons of modern warfare. Stay constantly alert to any indication that the enemy has used a biological agent. Don't panic!

8 - 7 First Aid Is Vital.

Now more than ever, it is necessary for the individual citizen know well those measures which can save his or her life and the lives of others. If you have not received prior training in the special measures required following exposure to biological agents, they may at first seem difficult to remember or difficult to do. Use this book as a reference and as an aid in getting them firmly fixed in your mind. In any case, be ready to rely on *yourself* when first aid is required, and your chances of survival will be greatly increased.

8 - 8 Biological Agents Can Be Neutralized.

It is possible to make biological agents lose their harmful effects and to remove contamination by procedures referred to as decontamination. Details of how you as an individual can accomplish decontamination are covered in later chapters. The knowledge that biological agents can be made ineffective should build confidence in your ability to continue your job in the presence of these agents.

8 - 9 Every North American Citizen Must Know.
- 1. The types of biological agents and their effects.
- 2. How biological agents can be detected.
- 3. How to use their protective equipment.
- 4. How to care for their protective equipment.
- 5. How to perform first aid.
- 6. How to remove biological agents from themselves and their equipment.

As a North American Citizen , you must master the six objectives listed above. Learning these objectives now will make the next chapters easier to read and understand. When you have mastered the six objectives listed, the payoff will justify your efforts. You and your community will then be prepared to perform your jobs against an enemy using biological <u>and chemical</u> agents. Such preparedness results when training, knowledge, confidence, and courage replace fear and panic.

CHAPTER 9

PROCEDURES IN BIOLOGICAL OPERATIONS
FM 21-41

9 - 1 Biological Operations Defined.

Biological agents are microorganisms that cause disease in man. A biological operation, then, is the employment of biological agents by a weapon system to produce casualties or damage. It is the intentional use of biological agents that makes biological operations different from natural disease hazards. Actually, everyone is waging a fight against microorganisms from the moment they are born. The eyes of an infant are disinfected shortly after birth to free them from dangerous microorganisms. At home the parents continue the fight against microorganisms by keeping their body and clothes clean, sterilizing milk and bottles, keeping them away from people with colds, and seeing that they get certain immunizations ("shots"). You will remember that at a very young age you were impressed with the importance of personal cleanliness, and probably before you entered school you were given a smallpox vaccination. ___Any belief that biological operations concern some unknown super weapon is based on fact. Mycoplasma fermentans (incognitus) used in the Gulf War is a prime example.___ Man's fight against disease-producing microorganisms has gone on since the beginning of time. Biological operations are simply a manmade attempt to produce disease on a large scale.

9 - 2 Characteristics Of Biological Agents.

Whereas some microorganisms cause such diseases as typhoid and cholera, others are used to produce antibiotics (penicillin, streptomycin, aureomycin, and others) that fight diseases. Most microorganisms are not harmful to man. Many industries today use certain desirable bacteria and fungi. Yeast, a group of fungi, is used in the manufacture of bread and beer. Molds, also fungi, are used in making vinegar and cheese and in such industries as textile manufacturing and leather tanning.

Only a few types of microorganisms produce disease. Even fewer types are so infective and so hardy that they can be used as biological agents.

- ◆ **1. Yersinia Pestis (Plague)**
- ◆ **2. Bacillus Anthracis (Anthrax)**
- ◆ **3. Vibrio Cholera (Cholera)**
- ◆ **4. Salmonella Typhi (Typhoid Fever)**

These four microorganisms, in this order, are the most likely candidates for use in a biological attack by a terrorist organization or nation, and are the ones that we will concentrate our defense and treatment against.

Since microorganisms are living matter, they behave as do other living things. They multiply, breath, eat, grow, and die. They depend on moisture, food, and certain limits of temperature for life and growth. When their surroundings do not provide suitable conditions, they die. Most microorganisms are killed by such simple acts as boiling, adding purification tablets to water, cooking food, or exposure to sunlight. They also can be removed with soap and water.

Biological agents can be released into the air to travel downwind as aerosols composed of tiny particles. These particles, which are smaller than dust particles, normally cannot be seen as they travel downwind and can go wherever dust can go. **Unless a protective mask is worn**, the biological agent particles will be inhaled and thus cause infection that can result in sickness or death. Biological agents can also contaminate food and water supplies and, in some cases, clothing and equipment. These agents may also be spread by vectors such as mosquitoes, fleas, flies, or ticks. Some of the biological agents may live in the target area for long periods of time; however, the majority will probably die in a few hours when exposed to sunlight.

9 - 3 Ways Of Killing Microorganisms
- 1. Boiling at least 15 minutes.
- 2. Water purification tablets.
- 3. Soap, scrubbing.
- 4. Sunning your clothes on a line.
- 5. Cooking.

Good defenses against biological agents.

Biological agents cannot be detected by your five senses or by chemical detectors. Their presence can be confirmed only by laboratory examination. Furthermore, biological agents do not produce immediate effects. The time between exposure to an agent and the beginning of disease symptoms (known as the incubation period) can vary from a few hours to several days, depending upon the agent used. Men exposed to equal amounts of an agent will react differently. Some may escape disease entirely, others may have very mild attacks, while others may become seriously ill.

9 - 4 How Biological Agents Get Into The Body

Most biological agents in aerosol form get into the body through the respiratory tract. Some agents may also be used to contaminate water or food and thus could enter your body if you drink the contaminated water or ate the contaminated food.

If your hands are contaminated, it is possible for you to transfer a biological agent to your mouth or to food you handle. If vectors are used to spread a biological agent, the agent would probably enter the body as a result of a vector bite.

Remember that although contaminated food or water and vector bites can permit biological agents to enter the body, **the main danger if there is a biological agent attack is breathing the agent aerosols. Your protective mask, if properly fitted, will prevent agents in the aerosol from entering your body.**

9 - 5 The Dangers Of Biological Operations.

Biological operations present dangers that you must be prepared to meet. Among the dangers are new ways of disseminating biological agents, and new agents that might be developed.

When a person coughs or sneezes, tiny drops of moisture are blown from his mouth and nose into the air. If he is ill, the spray may carry harmful microorganisms to other persons. Scientists working in laboratories have found that they are able to spread biological agents in much the same way -- in the form of an aerosol. **Thus, the microorganisms can be dispersed by special spray devices or by munitions designed to produce an aerosol upon impact.**

When microorganisms are disseminated in this manner, anyone who breathes the aerosol is likely to become infected. Aerosols normally will be invisible a few feet from the point of dissemination.

CHAPTER 10

FACTS YOU SHOULD KNOW ABOUT BIOLOGICAL OPERATIONS
FM 21-41

Biological agents are hard to detect and identify. There is no simple method of detecting biological agents, since they are tiny particles of living matter so small they can be seen only under a microscope. These tiny living particles are referred to as microorganisms.

Positive identification of a biological agent is more difficult than is the detection of the possible presence of such an agent. Positive identification may require from several days to weeks and can be made only by trained personnel. This is true, first, because it may be necessary to wait from a few days to weeks for symptoms of the disease to appear in infected persons. Second, laboratory analysis of material taken from sick individuals and a study of disease symptoms must be made before an agent can be identified. **You cannot see, feel, or taste microorganisms spread in a biological attack.**

Even though biological agents are hard to detect, you must do what you can to alert your community or a good Radio talk show host of an attack at the earliest possible moment. Every clue counts. A prompt report of suspicious clues or activities may lead to the prevention of many cases of illness and may even prevent deaths. You should inform your community leaders or local Health Department of any illness you or your friends have. Report at once any food or water suspected of making you ill.

The appearance of certain clues may warn you of, or cause you to suspect, a biological attack. You can assist in the detection by reporting to your community leaders the location of any of the following suspicious items or circumstances:

- 1 <u>Light aircraft (such as Cessna 150) dropping unidentified material or spraying unidentified substances.</u> Look closely at the landing gear strut for presence of a vapor trail.
- 2 New or unusual types of bombs, particularly those which burst with little or no blast.
- 3 <u>Smokes of unknown source or nature.</u>
- 4 <u>An increased occurrence of sick or dead animals.</u>
- 5 Unusual or unexplained increases in the number of insects, such as mosquitoes, ticks, or fleas.
- 6 Any weapon not seeming to have any immediate casualty effect.

CHAPTER 11

HOW TO PROTECT YOURSELF AGAINST BIOLOGICAL AGENTS

In the event of biological attack, you have several effective ways of protecting yourself.

11 - 1 Health

Guard your health by good diet, sleep, and exercise. A clean body and sanitary living area help prevent the spread of disease, regardless of its source.

11 - 2 Shots

Keep your immunizations up to date, <u>You should have your doctor give you a Pneumococcal Polysaccharide vaccination,</u> it will increase your body resistance to disease and may save your life.

11 - 3 Purity

Eat and drink from only approved sources. The enemy may try to contaminate food and water. Contaminated food or water can cause sickness or death.

11 - 4 Report

Be alert. Report suspicious activities to you local community leader. The enemy may use sabotage and other means of employing biological agents.

11 - 5 Cover

Microorganisms must enter your body to cause disease. <u>Your protective mask</u> and protective clothing properly worn will protect you.

11 - 6 Avoid

Avoid contaminated areas. You help the enemy if you catch and spread disease.

11 - 7 Scrub

Scrub hands and face with soap and water frequently. Take a complete bath as often as possible.

11 - 8 Sterilize

Clothing should be either boiled, scrubbed with soap and water, dry-cleaned, or aired in the sun.

11 - 9 Antibiotics

Purchase and have on hand as large a supply of the following as you can afford. May be obtained in quantities from farmers supply facilities (Quality Farm and Fleet, CO OP, LANDMARK, etc.).

AT LEAST:
- (a) One pound of TERRAMYCIN per person.
- (b) One pound of PANMYCIN per person.
- (c) 2 vials of AGRI-STREPT per person.
- (d) Four packages of TERRAMYCIN SOLUBLE POWDER per person.
- (e) 30 packages of either BIOLYTE CALF ELECTROLYTE FORMULA or ANCHOR ORAL REHYDRATION CALF REHYDRATION POWDER. (this is mandatory for the treatment of CHOLERA).

<u>Preparation of these antibiotics for human use will be covered in a following chapter.</u>

BACTERIOLOGICAL WARFARE

11 - 10 **Medical Supplies**
AT LEAST:

- (a) Three Glass 5 cc hypodermic syringes & needles .
- (b) 20 plastic disposable 5 cc hypodermic syringes & needles. May be obtained in quantities from farmers supply facilities (Quality Farm and Fleet, CO OP, LANDMARK, etc.).
- (c) One bottle Iodine Tincture.
- (d) One bottle isopropyl alcohol rubbing compound.
- (e) Two jugs of household bleach.
- (f) One oral thermometer.
- (g) One rectal thermometer. (for children).
- (h) Bag of sterile cotton balls.
- (i) One box of latex rubber exam gloves.
- (j) Several bars or bottles of a strong disinfection soap. Lye soap can be obtained at most army surplus store's (or you can make it) and is one of the best.
- (k) Two bottles of hydrogen peroxide per person.
- (l) One container of petroleum jelly. (For rectal thermometer).
- (m) At least 10 tyvek sack suit, with drawstring neck, elastic sleeve, air inlet, with shoes & hood. If these cannot be obtained, a motorcycle rain suite can be used and can be obtained at most cycle shops.
- (n) Four 117A8 Bags of 1000 00 Empty CAPSULES. Obtained from PROLONGEVITY, LTD 10 Alden Road Unit 6 Markham, Ontario L3R2S1 Canada. 1-800-544-4440
- (o) One 118A7 CAPSULE FILLING MACHINE FOR 00 CAPSULES. Obtained from PROLONGEVITY, LTD 10 Alden Road Unit 6 Markham, Ontario L3R2S1 Canada. 1-800-544-4440.
- (p) Five pounds of salt per person.

Remember -- The most important rules are
- (1) putting on your protective mask
- (2) avoiding food and water that could be contaminated
- (3) using soap and water generously
- (4) taking all prescribed immunizations or prophylactic antibiotics.

CHAPTER 12

GUARDING AGAINST CONTAMINATION
BACTERIAL & VIRAL

12 - 1

Thorough hand washing with soap and water before and after contact with any sick person, as well as any contact with potentially contaminated surfaces, is simple medical common sense. The Orientals have for centuries not touched strangers when greeting. Instead, they politely bow or place hands in a prayer like gesture demonstrating a recognition of the other person's presence. Military tradition, for as far back in time as one cares to go, dictated a non-touching hand salute. It could very well be that in cultures where touching was a routine gesture of stranger greeting and recognition, the hand-shakers and the "touchy-feely" peoples died from infectious diseases that were easily spread by hand contact, leaving behind cultures that didn't touch to survive and populate those areas. It would be to our advantage that in the future North American Citizens adopted a non-touching hand salute to reduce the possible spread of disease.

12 - 2

If administering aid to a citizen that may have been exposed to a biological agent, one should wear latex rubber gloves. Especially if one is going to deal with any blood, secretions, body fluids, or any article that has been soiled by them.

12 - 3

Any environmental surface contaminated by body fluids, blood, vomit, saliva, bowl movements, or other bodily secretions should be cleaned up immediately or avoided. The fluids should be placed in an air tight plastic bag and incinerated. The surface or article should then be cleaned with a disinfectant. At least one part household bleach to nine parts water should be sufficient. Be aware of cross contamination. Any object that has been in contact with the fluid should also be considered to be contaminated. If the body fluid splatters on clothing, remove the clothing or soak it with a disinfectant.

12 - 4

If you are near anyone who is coughing and not wearing a mask or cannot be compelled to wear a mask, then you should wear a mask when in close proximity to them.

12 - 5

Protective eye-wear should be worn in any situation wherein a splatter of blood, bloody secretions or body fluids are possible.

12 - 6

Any bedding, towels, or clothing used or touched by the infected should be washed in hot, bleached, soapy water before being used by anyone else.

BACTERIOLOGICAL WARFARE

12 - 7

Do not use or reuse any sharp instruments, needles, or syringes that have come in contact with another person. If you are required to handle such instruments, be extremely cautious not to cut your skin or puncture yourself with them. If someone loans you a needle or tweezers to remove a sliver or piece of glass from the skin, sterilize it by passing the tool through a flame or by soaking it for at least 15 minutes in a strong disinfectant. Glass hypodermic syringes & reusable needles, scalpel, tweezers, and other sterilizeable medical instruments may be sterilized in a common household pressure cooker. Place one cup of water in the bottom of the cooker, then insert the rack that accompany most household pressure cookers, and then place the instruments to be sterilized upon the rack. Cover, and set on moderate heat. Start counting when the steam jiggle starts to move. Time for 30 minutes -- this will kill even the most resistant spores of anthrax and all viruses.

12 - 8

Do not share eating utensils with a person you suspect has been exposed to a biological agent or to be a carrier as in the case of typhoid. Do not allow them access to your food whereby their secretions, open sores, or blood could contaminate your food. Avoid any food handling institutions where you cannot vouch personally for the employees. Be very discriminating as to where you eat. Observe the employees in the restaurant you routinely visit. If they appear unhealthy, consider an alternative eating establishment.

If you are eating in a restaurant, insure that the food is steaming when it is served to you. Dining out is not without risk especially where persons who are infected with an biological agent and other food borne infectious diseases are possibly employed. You must assume that the employees are infected until medical tests prove otherwise. Make certain that the utensils are clean and the food has been prepared recently and is still fresh. Cold salads, peeled fruit dishes, cream dishes, open public access salad bars, cold food counters, and buffets have always been dangerous propositions in foreign countries, and as the infectious disease rates increase in this country similar considerations will apply depending upon the locale and the prevalence of infectious persons.

Most credible diarrhea disease experts recommend that you not eat food unless it is steaming hot when it arrives at the table. This will insure that the food was raised once to the boiling point. This amount of heat will destroy many protozoa, bacteria, and viruses. Unfortunately, however, it is not sufficient to destroy anthrax spores and it is not to be considered a sterilization process as some organisms will only be killed by prolonged high temperatures. It has been said that frying a food thoroughly adequately sterilizes it.

Avoid under cooked seafood, especially when cholera has been reported to be in the area. Under no circumstances eat any under cooked sea food that you suspect may have come from the Gulf of Mexico as this area already has an established cholera foci. Avoid sauces prepared with raw eggs (mayonnaise, hollandaise, etc.) as eggs are a source of salmonella. Food that has remained at room temperature for a prolonged time, even though re-refrigerated, is a good candidate for contamination. The common practice whereby a person licks a spoon and then uses it to take contents out of a food container contaminates the food container with the microorganisms from his/her mouth. Avoid condiments (Catsup, mustard, hot sauces, etc.) in restaurants that allow for communal use because one never knows with whom one is communing.

BACTERIOLOGICAL WARFARE

If food is catered, evaluate the hygiene and risk group status of persons who prepare the food. It is not unreasonable to refuse a plate that has thumb prints on the eating surface or that has visible evidence of finger traffic. Dishes which predispose a number of persons to dip into with crackers, chips or bread can become contaminated when people take additional dips with the same piece of food that has touched their mouth.

If the need arises, a pressure cooker provides sufficient sterilizing capacity for any food, utensil, or dressing.

12 - 9

If your school district does not have an exclusion policy of not permitting children with a known communicable disease to attend school, and in times of a epidemic, (whether it is the flu or plague), of not having a school nurse on every school bus checking each and every student before they can board the bus, and not having another school nurse at every accessible entrance to the school checking every student before they can enter the school, and sending home any student with a suspected communicable disease, then one of the following must be considered:

- ◆ (1) Keep your children home.
- ◆ (2) Transfer him/her to a school district that does have an enforced exclusion policy.
- ◆ (3) **Consider home schooling.**
- ◆ (4) Insist that your children wear a full face respirator, and a full body protective garment. Instruct your children that if any Teacher, Principle, School Administrator, or student, demand that their child remove the respirator and protective garment, get up and leave immediately. Assure your child that you will back him/her to the limit.

Do not tolerate your children being exposed to infected children in day-care centers, preschools, elementary schools, or even high schools. Educate your children in the recognition and avoidance of secretion passing behavior. Some parents think it is cute to have their children going around hugging and kissing other children. If the kissing child is the product of an infected parent not yet obviously ill, this behavior can pass any number of diseases. Don't allow strangers to kiss or handle your children unless you are reasonably certain of their health.

The overly affectionate day-care attendant or the kindly person who gains pleasure from kissing every child they come in contact with has a higher probability of carrying an infectious organism due to that behavior.   Increased contact enhances their chances of acquiring transmissible diseases.

12 - 10

If you or a loved-one is placed in a hospital room, nursing home, or adult day-care center with a plague, typhoid fever, AIDS, or cholera patient, insist upon being moved to a different room. By proper disease control requirements, patients with infectious diseases should be isolated. If your hospital does not isolate those patients, then it is your duty to insist upon reverse isolation by being moved. It is probably not in your best interest to frequent or be admitted to hospitals. (Unless appropriate precautions are taken).

Consider carefully the risk group status of the doctors, nurses, or ancillary personnel who come in contact with your body while you are in a hospital. If they appear ill, are coughing, or otherwise appear ill with infectious disease, consult with your doctor. Ensure that when people touch your mucous membranes, open wounds, or objects that will contact your body, that they are wearing clean rubber or plastic gloves and observe sterile technique.

BACTERIOLOGICAL WARFARE

12 - 11

Be careful where you bathe, share hot tubs, and even where you swim. Don't bathe in lakes or ponds, unless the facility maintains the water at an optimal chloride level and keeps the surfaces disinfected between patrons. Any layer of slimy scum on the walls or sides of the tub is probably composed of sloughed skin or body fluids. Be concerned. The Plague bacterium can live in aqueous environments from 2 to 30 days. Hot, moist places are excellent locations where the other infectious diseases people carry can be spread.

12 - 12

If your children are playing with other children whose parents are high risk group members, or known to be infected, then stop that behavior. Don't make a big issue out of it; just carefully explain to them that you don't want them to play with that child any longer. If you want to be certain, then ask the parents of that child to have the child and themselves tested. (Remember, a person can become a carrier of the typhoid bacterium, the causative agent of typhoid fever, with out showing any signs of being a carrier). Once you have seen the results, then you can resume contact with some measure of safety.

Teach children how to properly limit exposure to infectious diseases. Raise them to politely curtsy, bow, or make a gesture of greeting without shaking hands with strangers. Reserve this gesture for those persons with whom a genuine bond is necessary and where the probability of infectious disease is low. A significant percentage of the common cold and influenza are assumed to be transmitted in this fashion.

Children should be constantly reminded not to touch their mouths, noses, or eyes unless they have washed their hands, and to avoid persons who are coughing, spitting, or bleeding unless they are properly equipped with gloves, and masks or face shields.

Educate your children to identify the presence of open sores (cutaneous anthrax) on other children or adults and to specifically avoid contact with persons with these lesions. Examine discretely your children's playmates for lesions, sores, or scabs. Any sign of illness is enough to prevent contact until it can be established that they are not due to infectious causes.

Teach them to immediately wash their hands it they contact the saliva or deposited mucous of others (such as touching a drinking fountain where someone has spit or a school desk where previously chewed gum or "boogers" have been sequestered). Encourage nose blowing so that contents of the nose are expelled after aerosolized particulate matter is trapped in the mucous and discourage the practice of "sniffing" wherein the contents of the nose are ingested by rapidly inhaling through the nose with the mouth closed. It only insures that bacteria gain access to deeper nasal passages. Teach them to keep their mouths off of railings, drinking fountains, and objects frequently touched by the public. Be especially careful about what they touch when in the rest room. If your child acquires a disease in any of these manners, you can bet it will be brought into your home.

Children should be instructed how to recognize and **not touch** medical equipment containing waste (syringes, iv tubing, wastes, etc.)

12 - 13

There are those who wish to take chances by sharing drinks, kissing, or having close contact with patients. That does not make the behavior safe. Unprotected close contact should be avoided, especially by anyone with a compromised immune system.

12 - 14

Take precautions against hematophagous (blood sucking) insects. A valid recommendation is to wear insect repellent and protective clothing (Tyvec sack suit, drawstring neck, elastic sleeve, air inlet, with shoes & hood), body guard latex examination gloves. Wear long shirt & pants with high top boots, with the pants tucked inside the boots, and gloves. Then take flea collars and place around ankles and wrist, making sure that the flea collar does not come into contact with bare skin. In light of the fact fleas transmit plague, a valid recommendation would be to not take care of flea bearing animals of uncertain health status. Recall that the greatest plague known to man was spread by fleas.

Certain species of fleas prefer to live on humans and jump on other people to take blood meals. Whenever going into some environment that is particularly frequented by the type of persons who has fleas (and one does not have his tyvec sack suit handy), tucking one's pant-legs into one's socks can help prevent the fleas from getting to the legs. If circumstances cause you to sleep in a bed where others have recently slept, consider wearing insect repellent.

Be especially careful about letting your children contact other children who may have lice. These are blood sucking creatures and their mouth parts must be assumed to be contaminated with blood borne pathogens (especially plague & AIDS) and capable of transmitting disease. If you notice a child with multiple flea bites around the belt line or the sock area investigate the possibility and discourage your child from playing with that child or allowing that child access to your home. If you notice your child with multiple flea bites, assume that your child **has** been exposed to plague and start immediate treatment with tetracycline.

12 - 15

Do not allow any potentially contaminated object to pierce your skin. Common sources of infection such as ear piercing with a community needle, non sterile acupuncture, or any sharp object that has been shared by someone else without adequate sterilization could prove lethal.

It is a common secretive practice among children to become "blood brothers". Be certain to educate your children that this should not be done. They should also be taught to avoid contact with blood, mucous, saliva, vomit, or soiled articles.

12 - 16

Educate your children and the people around you not to have sexual or secretions sharing activities without thoroughly knowing their companions health backgrounds. This requires them not to kiss or be kissed by risk group members and especially sexually promiscuous persons. (Plague, typhoid, cholera, are very efficiently spread by kissing) and not to have physical contact with sores, cuts, or scrapes of others. "Kissing the boo-boo better" could make you worse.

12 - 17

Employ discrimination in whom you choose to be closely associated with. Ensure to the best of your ability that the persons with whom you may be forced to contact are free of plague, cholera, typhoid, and anthrax.

Consider carefully the risk benefit ratio of mouth - to - mouth resuscitation and with whom you would be willing to take that risk. Surely your wife or child is a reasonable risk, but a sickly looking stranger is another case altogether.

BACTERIOLOGICAL WARFARE

12 - 18

When travel requirements make the use of public rest rooms unavoidable, practice infection control techniques that assume the objects are contaminated with infectious organisms-because they are! Scientific studies have shown that simply flushing toilets and urinals cause the infectious organisms to be come airborne in a fine mist. When touching rest room doors, sink fixtures, flush handles, toilet seats, door handles or other objects be extremely careful and cognizant that they are more likely than any other surfaces to contain infectious organisms that are found in high concentrations on the genitals.

When ever possible use your feet to open doors (most doors can be opened at least one way with a kick) or manipulate objects such as toilet lids or handles. Carry your own toilet paper reserves for those instances when the facility is particularly seedy or the paper has visible evidence of water marks or has been resting on a filthy surface. Remember, you will be applying that paper directly to your rectal mucous membranes which often are prone to bleed due to abrasions, fissures, or hemorrhoids that allow direct access to your blood stream.

When making bowel movements into water filled toilets, prevent the refluxing splash caused by pieces of fecal material hitting the water from contacting you. Consider that the water hitting your rectum contains microscopic quantities of the contents of the bowl from the bowels of persons that used the toilet before you. Cholera, an acute infectious gastrointestinal disease, is profuse with watery diarrhea in which large quantities of vibro comma organisms are shed. If these organisms are introduced into your rectum the disease cholera may result. The same holds true for typhoid fever, plague and to a lesser extent anthrax. These germs are applied directly to the inside of your body with every splash.

Anyone who has ever had diarrhea knows that when they flush, sometimes the large visible floating particles do not go down. That same effect is occurring with respect to unseen microscopic organisms. Flushing before using the toilet will reduce this effect by dilution but is incomplete, this problem can be more adequately approached by extending a length of toilet paper across the seat in a sling-like manner so that the falling momentum and the impact of the bowl movement hitting the water is reduced by the fecal material hitting the paper. Also, one can adjust one's position to deposit the bowel movement to a portion of the bowl that causes it to hit the bowl rather than the deep water portion; however, be also careful not to allow portions of your anatomy to touch the filthy areas of the toilet.

Often men's penises (if sufficiently endowed) touch the most forward portion of the toilet bowl where drippings from prior use collect. When the genitals touch this area they become contaminated with the previous user's body fluids. (salmonella typhosa the causative agent of typhoid fever is shed in the urine in large numbers during the early stages of typhoid fever).

Whenever possible use a disposable paper seat liner or disinfectant and carry a spare in your automobile while traveling or to work if you feel the probability is likely that such precautions are necessary.

If objects are touched in situations such as this or other situations in which there is a high probability that human body fluids have been in contact, be very careful not to touch any part of your body, especially the mucous membranes or the eyes, nose, mouth, or genitals until thoroughly washing your hands. After washing your hands in a public rest room, use the paper that you dried your hands with to turn faucets, flush handles or open doors.

12 - 19

Consider the reality that whenever a sick person enters your home and uses your facilities (especially your toilet) they contaminate the bathtub, toilet, and sink. Keep your home and toilet facilities clean. Make sure you disinfect your toilet bowls or bathtubs after others use them. People who use your toilet deposit the contents of their bowels into your living space. If possible, keep one bathroom for guests use and the other for your own private use and frequently clean the guest facility, especially after someone who appears to be ill or a member of a risk group was likely to be in attendance. If you are selective about the people who enter your home, you can limit your exposure. If in the aftermath of a party where numerous persons of uncertain infectious carriage have used your facilities, then use a satisfactory disinfectant on the toilet bowl, sink, or bath tub.

12 - 20

When using a locker room, public pool, or shower facility be very careful not to allow your wet feet to touch your clothing that will eventually touch your body. Of most common concern are your socks, the lining of your underwear (quite often people catch their feet on the inside lining of their underwear when putting them on), bathing suit, or pants. This is an excellent way of depositing anthrax spores onto the genital area, (the mortality of untreated cutaneous anthrax ranges up to 25%).

Do not allow your clothing to touch the floor when dressing in a locker room or sitting on a toilet. If you do, you are in essence painting your body with whatever slimy secretions that were deposited there by the numerous persons whose "aim" was poor. Remember, the bacterium that causes typhoid fever can be passed in urine.

12 - 21

Do not wear other peoples clothing without proper washing in hot, bleached, soapy water because that is how human insect parasites are passed.

The wearing of gloves will probably be of increased benefit and style in the future. In the 19 century, a woman of means would not consider venturing into public without gloves. The city dwelling woman of the future will probably come to realize that same concern expressed in the past was one of infectious disease -- necessity translated into style.

12 - 22

Don't use lipstick, make-up, ointments, or chap-stick that has been used by others. In each, you are applying a media that can harbor and preserve microbes.

Use of communal make-up applicators should be avoided. Think of what actually happens when one teenager picks a pimple, draws blood, then covers the blemish with a powder brush. As she hands the powder brush to her blemished friend, she is transferring blood and serum to be applied to the open pores and similar blood contaminated pimple lesions of her "friend." Such sharing friends better be prepared to share their diseases namely plague, and anthrax.

12 - 23

Consider that in large public gatherings an excellent opportunity for a terrorist to release a biological agent exists. Dust could conceal the spores of anthrax and airborne plague bacteria.

BACTERIOLOGICAL WARFARE

If you breath that dust you are allowing those organisms to take up residence in your airways. Consider donning your full face mask (gas mask) if you choose to attend such gatherings. At the very least obtain a flexible, surgical mask that can easily conform to the contours of the face for use in such situations. The rigid, monkey face type mask are inadequate if air is breathed around the edges. By blowing one's nose and looking at the contents of the discharge, one can tell if particulate matter is being filtered out or ingested when you swallow the liquid from the back of your nose during a "sniffle." You would do well to remember that gastrointestinal plague or anthrax is 99.9% fatal.

12 - 24

When using public transportation, be selective about who you sit next to and where you sit. If you are seated next to a person who is coughing, don't consider how that person will feel if you get up and sit somewhere else. Consider how you will feel in the next few days when you acquire the same infection that person has probably acquired through airborne route.

Understand also that bacteria particles that are applied to the sick person's hands when he wipes his nose or coughs are also transferred to every surface that the person touches. When you touch the same surfaces, the bacteria particles get on your hands and come in contact with your mucous membranes when you touch your eyes, nose, or mouth.

12 - 25

A reliance on individual water purification systems for drinking water is a must, especially in those areas where sanitary standards are low. In cities that rely upon treated water, certain spore forming microbes (anthrax) are resistant to chlorination and would be a good choice of biological agents to use in a sabotage operation. As the number of water-borne infections available to terrorist organization increase, it will be increasingly difficult to prevent them from contaminating the water systems.

12 - 26

Excess Iron Increases Risk Of Infection. Excess iron not only serves as a growth essential metal for microbial cells, but also suppresses the bodies immune system. Iron catalyzes formation of hydroxyl radicals that can damage normal host cells by initiating autoxidation chain processes, by adding oxygen at double bonds, by abstracting hydrogen from allyl carbon atoms, and by oxidizing sulfhydryl, thioether, and amino functions.

Components Of The Iron-Withholding Defense System:

The abundance of iron and its wide redox potential make this metal useful as a catalytic center for a broad spectrum of metabolic functions. However, these attributes render the metal dangerous to manipulate. Living matter has a variety of strategies for dealing with this dilemma. For example, man has developed various means to obtain useful concentrations of the metal, to exclude and seclude dangerous quantities, and to withhold growth-essential amounts from invaders. When one comes down with a fever, the body is releasing components into the blood that will tie up nearly all available iron and store it in the liver, where it will not be available to invading microbes.

Challenges To The System

Notwithstanding the remarkable efficacy of your iron-withholding defense system, hosts do develop bacterial infections. The following conditions can overload our bodies with iron and can lead to disease.

(1) Excessive intake of iron via intestinal absorption.
- (a) Excessive consumption of red meats (heme iron). The old wives tale about eating chicken soup or broth to treat a fever really works.
- (b) Adulteration of processed foods with inorganic iron.
- (c) Use of iron cookware.
- (d) Excessive intake of ethanol (HCL secretion enhanced).
- (e) Ingestion of ascorbic acid with inorganic iron.

(2) Inhaled iron.
- (a) Tobacco smoking (1.2ug of iron per cigarette pack)

(3) Substitution of bovine milk (cow) or milk formula for human milk in nutrition of human nursling.

Yersiniosis (plague) and Vibrio cholera are far more prominent in patients who have overloaded their bodies with iron.

CHAPTER 13

Preparation of Veterinary & Agriculture Antibiotics for Human Use.

13 - 1 Most Likely Used Microbes in Biological Warfare

These four microorganisms, in this order, are the most likely candidates for use in a biological attack. Therefore, these are the ones we will concentrate on for defense and treatment.
- 1. Yersinia Pestis (Plague)
- 2. Bacillus Anthracis (Anthrax)
- 3. Vibrio Cholera (Cholera)
- 4. Salmonella Typhi (Typhoid Fever)

13 - 2 Antibiotics

These antibiotics are effective treatment for **Yersinia pestis, Vibro cholera, Salmonella typhi, and Mycoplasma fermentans (incognitos).**
- Panmycin 500 (Bolus) Pneumonia And Scours Treatment (Tetracycline Hydrochloride)
- Terramycin Scours Tablets (Oxytetracycline HCl)
- Terramycin Soluble Powder #4163 (Oxytetracycline HCl)
- Terramycin-343 Soluble Powder (Oxytetracycline HCl) #5632
- Oxy-Tet 100 (Oxytetracycline HCl)
- Agri-Strept (Sterile Penicillin G Procaine and Dihydrostreptomycin Sulfate) (Penicillin is effective treatment for Bacillus Anthracis.) <u>(Terramycin & Panmycin can be used in people allergic to penicillin. **Do not use Penicillin in combination with Terramycin or Panmycin.)**</u>

13 - 3 **Panmycin 500 Pneumonia And Scours Treatment (Tetracycline Hydrochloride)** may

be obtained in quantities from farmers supply facilities (Quality Farm and Fleet, CO OP, LANDMARK, etc.). Panmycin is sold for pneumonia and scours treatment and states on the label that it is not for human use. The panmycin contained in these bolus tablets and that from a pharmacy <u>is identical.</u> These **Veterinary panmycin bolus** tablets are deliberately made too large for human use -- 1. 1/5 inches long, 3/5 inch wide, 1/2 inch deep. <u>In order for this antibiotic to be used, it must be reduced to a powder.</u>

First you need to obtain a grain mill, coffee grinder etc. One of the finest compact & versatile grain mills I have tested, The Back To Basics grain mill can be obtained from NITRO-PACK PREPAREDNESS CENTER 151 North Main St. Heber City Utah 84032 1-800-866-4876 Priced at $64.95. It also can be obtained from Lehmans Hardware and Appliances One Lehman Circle, PO Box 41 Kidron, Ohio 44636 (USA) 1-216-857-5757, Fax 1-216-857-5785 Priced At $75.95. A good quality food blender will also work. Vita Mix is the best available and can be acquired from a good health food store or catalogue.

Second you will need a pestle. A 1/4 inch by 6 inch dowel rod may be used. One of the best we have tested is a bullet starter used by muzzle loader enthusiasts. This has a round wooden ball with a short brass rod and a 1/4 inch by six inch dowel rod with a brass tip. It may be obtained at most sporting shops for around $5. This will be used to help the crushed

Panmycin feed through the grain mill. (this is not required if you have a good quality Vita-Mix food blender.)

Third you will need a pair of channel locks or vice grips. These can be obtained at any automotive supply.

13 - 4 Procedure

First attach the grain mill to a counter top or table. Next take a Panmycin bolus tablet and place it length wise in the jaws of the channel locks or vice grips. Crush and allow the pieces to fall into the grain mill hopper. While turning the grain mill handle push the crushed pieces into the grain mill burr. (You will find it easier if you loosen the knob on the grain mill handle. This will allow bigger pieces to feed.) The panmycin is reduced to a fine powder. (With the Vita-Mix you just pour the large pills into the blender and turn it on).

An RCBS 5-0-5 powder scale makes an good scale for weighing out antibiotic dosage and can be obtained from most reloading shops for about $45, these scales measure in GRAINS.

13.5 PANMYCIN BOLUS DOSAGE

DOSAGE DETERMINED BY BODY WEIGHT, REFER TO THE FOLLOWING CHART

POUNDS OF BODY WEIGHT	TEASPOON	OUNCE	GRAMS	GRAINS
10	0.15	0.021	0.59	9
20	0.3	0.041	1.18	18
30	0.45	0.062	1.8	27
40	0.6	0.082	2.5	36
50	0.75	0.1	2.94	45
60	0.9	0.12	3.52	54
70	1.05	0.14	4.11	63
80	1.2	0.16	4.7	72
90	1.35	0.19	5.3	81
100	1.5	0.21	5.8	90
110	1.65	0.22	6.46	99
120	1.8	0.25	7.1	108
130	1.95	0.27	7.6	117
140	2.1	0.29	8.2	126
150	2.25	0.31	8.8	135
160	2.4	0.32	9.4	144
170	2.55	0.35	9.99	153
180	2.7	0.37	10.58	162
190	2.85	0.39	11.17	171
200	3	0.41	11.76	180
210	3.15	0.43	12.34	189
220	3.3	0.45	12.9	198
230	3.45	0.47	13.52	207
240	3.6	0.49	14.1	216

- (1) ONCE, BEFORE YOU ENTER AN AREA THAT YOU ARE AT A HEIGHTENED RISK OF EXPOSURE TO THE ABOVE MICROBES, AND ONCE AFTER YOU HAVE LEFT THAT AREA, IF LESS THAN 16 HOURS SINCE EXPOSURE.
- (2) IF YOU HAVE BEEN EXPOSED TO THE ABOVE MICROBES: TWICE DAILY FOR TEN DAYS FOR PLAGUE, CHOLERA, AND TYPHOID FEVER. TWICE DAILY FOR TEN DAYS FOR ANTHRAX, THEN 1/2 INDICATED DOSAGE FOR AN ADDITIONAL 20 DAYS, THEN 1/4 OF INDICATED DOSAGE FOR 30 MORE DAYS.
- (3) FOUR TIMES DAILY FOR TEN DAYS -- AGGRESSIVE TREATMENT OF SEVERELY ILL PATIENTS.

Take the 118A7 capsule filling machine (see 11 - 10 Medical Supplies), insert the 117A8 00 Empty Capsules, and fill with the Panmycin powder. Each **LEVEL TEA SPOON = 6 CAPSULES**

An alternative would be to weigh out the panmycin powder and mix with a small amount of water, (about enough for a swallow), and chase with a glass of water. For children you can take a small glass of water, add the panmycin and a teaspoon of brown sugar. If the children object to the taste panmycin can also be mixed with a glass of CLUB SODA brought to room temperature, and swallowed swiftly. If a person starts hearing a ringing sound in the ears decrease dosage. (You will thank your lucky stars that you purchased the capsule machine and capsules so that this method could be avoided)

13 - 6 Terramycin Scours Tablets (Oxytetracycline HCl) may be obtained in quantities from farmers supply facilities (Quality Farm and Fleet, CO OP, LANDMARK, etc.). Terramycin is sold for bacterial enteritis and bacterial pneumonia treatment and states on the label that it is not for human use. The terramycin contained in these bolus tablets and that from a pharmacy is identical. These **Veterinary terramycin bolus** tablets are deliberately made too large for human use (1.1 inch long, .5 inch wide, .4 inch deep.) In order for this antibiotic to be used, it must be ground to a powder.

First you need to obtain a grain mill, or coffee grinder, etc. One of the finest compact & versatile grain mills we've tested, The Back To Basics grain mill, can be obtained from NITRO-PACK PREPAREDNESS CENTER 151 North Main St. Heber City Utah 84032 1-800-866-4876 Priced at $64.95. It also can be obtained from Lehmans Hardware and Appliances One Lehman Circle, PO Box 41 Kidron, Ohio 44636 (USA) 1-216-857-5757, Fax 1-216-857-5785 Priced At $75.95. (This is not required if you have a Vita Mix food blender.)

Second you will need a pestle. A 1/4 inch by 6 inch dowel rod may be used. One of the best we have tested is a bullet starter used by muzzle loader enthusiasts. This has a round wooden ball with a short brass rod and a 1/4 inch by six inch dowel rod with a brass tip. It may be obtained at most sporting shops for around $5. This will be used to help the crushed Panmycin feed through the grain mill. (this is not required if you have a Vita-Mix food blender.)

Third you will need a pair of channel locks or vice grips. These can be obtained at any automotive supply.

13 - 7 Procedure

First attach the grain mill to a counter top or table. Next take a Terramycin bolus tablet and place it length wise in the jaws of the channel locks or vice grips. Crush and allow the pieces to fall into the grain mill hopper. While turning the grain mill handle push the crushed pieces into the grain mill burr. (You will find it easier if you loosen the knob on the grain mill handle. This will allow bigger pieces to feed.) The terramycin is reduced to a fine powder. (With the Vita-Mix you just pour the large pills into the blender and turn it on).

An RCBS 5-0-5 powder scale makes an good scale for weighing out antibiotic dosage and can be obtained from most reloading shops for about $45, these scales measure in GRAINS.

13 - 8 TERRAMYCIN BOLUS DOSAGE

DOSAGE DETERMINED BY BODY WEIGHT, REFER TO THE FOLLOWING CHART

POUNDS OF BODY WEIGHT	TEASPOON	OUNCE	GRAMS	GRAINS
10	0.14	0.012	0.35	5.3
20	0.29	0.024	0.69	10.6
30	0.43	0.036	1.04	15.9
40	0.57	0.048	1.38	21.1
50	0.71	0.060	1.72	26.4
60	0.86	0.072	2.07	31.7
70	1.00	0.085	2.41	37
80	1.14	0.097	2.76	42.3
90	1.29	0.108	3.09	47.6
100	1.43	0.119	3.45	52.9
110	1.57	0.133	3.79	58.1
120	1.71	0.145	4.14	63.4
130	1.86	0.157	4.49	68.7
140	2.00	0.169	4.83	74
150	2.14	0.181	5.18	79.3
160	2.29	0.193	5.52	84.6
170	2.43	0.205	5.90	89.9
180	2.57	0.217	6.21	95.1
190	2.72	0.229	6.56	100.4
200	2.90	0.240	6.9	105.7
210	3.00	0.254	7.3	111
220	3.14	0.265	7.6	116
230	3.30	0.278	7.9	121.6
240	3.43	0.290	8.3	126.9

- (1) ONCE, BEFORE YOU ENTER AN AREA WHERE YOU ARE AT A HEIGHTENED RISK OF EXPOSURE TO THE ABOVE MICROBES, AND ONCE AFTER YOU HAVE LEFT THAT AREA, IF LESS THAN 16 HOURS SINCE EXPOSURE.
- (2) IF YOU HAVE BEEN EXPOSED TO THE ABOVE MICROBES: TWICE DAILY FOR TEN DAYS FOR PLAGUE, CHOLERA, AND TYPHOID FEVER. TWICE DAILY FOR TEN DAYS

FOR ANTHRAX, THEN 1/2 INDICATED DOSAGE FOR AN ADDITIONAL 20 DAYS, THEN 1/4 OF INDICATED DOSAGE FOR 30 MORE DAYS.
- (3) FOUR TIMES DAILY FOR TEN DAYS -- AGGRESSIVE TREATMENT OF SEVERELY ILL PATIENTS

Take the 118A7 capsule filling machine (see 11 - 10 Medical Supplies), insert the 117A8 00 Empty Capsules, and fill with the Panmycin powder. Each **LEVEL TEA SPOON = 6 CAPSULES**

An alternative would be to weigh out the terramycin powder and mix with a small amount of water, (about enough for a swallow), and chase with a glass of water. For children you can take a small glass of water, add the terramycin and a teaspoon of brown sugar. If the children object to the taste terramycin can also be mixed with a glass of CLUB SODA brought to room temperature, and swallowed swiftly. If a person starts hearing a ringing sound in the ears decrease dosage. (You will thank your lucky stars that you purchased the capsule machine and capsules so that this method could be avoided)

13 - 9 TERRAMYCIN SOLUBLE POWDER 10 grams of oxytetracycline HCl per 6.4 ounces (181.4 grams) #4163 (Oxytetracycline HCl) may be obtained in quantities from farmers supply facilities (Quality Farm and Fleet, CO OP, LANDMARK, etc.). Terramycin is sold for bacterial enteritis and bacterial pneumonia treatment and states on the label that it is not for human use. The terramycin contained in this soluble powder and that from a pharmacy is identical. It has the advantage of being in a powder form and does not have to be ground like the Terramycin Scours bolus tablets. However, each level teaspoon provides approximately 200 mg of terramycin compared to 350 mg per teaspoon for the Terramycin Scours bolus tablets.

13 - 10 TERRAMYCIN SOLUBLE POWDER DOSAGE #4163

DOSAGE DETERMINED BY BODY WEIGHT, REFER TO THE FOLLOWING CHART

BODY WEIGHT	TEASPOON	OUNCE	GRAMS	GRAINS
10	0.65	0.056	1.61	24.5
20	1.35	0.11	3.2	49.0
30	1.98	0.17	4.8	73.6
40	2.63	0.22	6.38	98.0
50	3.3	0.28	7.97	122.4
60	4	0.33	9.59	147
70	4.64	0.39	11.13	171.6
80	5.27	0.45	12.7	188
90	6	0.50	14.3	221.0
100	6.6	0.56	15.9	245
110	7.3	0.61	17.5	269.5
120	7.9	0.66	18.6	294
130	8.64	0.73	20.9	300.5
140	9.3	0.80	22.4	343
150	9.9	0.84	24.1	368

160	10.6	0.90	25.7	392.2
170	11.3	0.95	27.4	416.8
180	11.9	1.01	28.9	441
190	12.6	1.06	30.42	466
200	13.5	1.11	32.0	490
210	14.0	1.18	34	515
220	14.3	1.23	35.3	538
230	15.4	1.3	36.6	564
240	15.9	1.33	38.5	589

- (1) ONCE, BEFORE YOU ENTER AN AREA WHERE YOU ARE AT A HEIGHTENED RISK OF EXPOSURE TO THE ABOVE MICROBES, AND ONCE AFTER YOU HAVE LEFT THAT AREA, IF LESS THAN 16 HOURS SINCE EXPOSURE.
- (2) IF YOU HAVE BEEN EXPOSED TO THE ABOVE MICROBES: TWICE DAILY FOR TEN DAYS FOR PLAGUE, CHOLERA, AND TYPHOID FEVER. TWICE DAILY FOR TEN DAYS FOR ANTHRAX, THEN 1/2 INDICATED DOSAGE FOR AN ADDITIONAL 20 DAYS, THEN 1/4 OF INDICATED DOSAGE FOR 30 MORE DAYS.
- (3) FOUR TIMES DAILY FOR TEN DAYS -- AGGRESSIVE TREATMENT OF SEVERELY ILL PATIENTS

Take the 118A7 capsule filling machine Insert the 117A8 00 Empty Capsules and fill with the Terramycin powder. Each **LEVEL TEA SPOON = 6 CAPSULES**

An alternative would be to weigh out the terramycin powder and mix with a small amount of water, (about enough for a swallow), and chase with a glass of water. For children you can take a small glass of water, add the terramycin and a teaspoon of brown sugar. If the children object to the taste terramycin can also be mixed with a glass of CLUB SODA brought to room temperature, and swallowed swiftly. If a person starts hearing a ringing sound in the ears decrease dosage. (You will thank your lucky stars that you purchased the capsule machine and capsules so that this method could be avoided)

13 - 11 TERRAMYCIN SOLUBLE POWDER-343 102.4 grams of oxytetracycline HCl per 4.78 ounces #5632 (Oxytetracycline HCl) may be obtained in quantities from farmers supply facilities (Quality Farm and Fleet, CO OP, LANDMARK, etc.). Terramycin is sold for bacterial enteritis and bacterial pneumonia treatment and states on the label that it is not for human use. The terramycin contained in this soluble powder and that from a pharmacy is identical. It has the advantage of being in a powder form and does not have to be ground like the Terramycin Scours bolus tablets. However, each level teaspoon of #5632 provides approximately 1025 mg of terramycin compared to 350 mg per teaspoon for the Terramycin Scours bolus tablets.

13 - 12 **TERRAMYCIN SOLUBLE POWDER-343 DOSAGE #5632**

DOSAGE DETERMINED BY BODY WEIGHT, REFER TO THE FOLLOWING CHART

BODY WEIGHT	TEASPOON	OUNCE	GRAMS	GRAINS
10	0.05	0.004	0.12	1.79
20	0.10	0.008	0.23	3.6
30	0.145	0.012	0.35	5.37
40	0.19	0.016	0.46	7.15
50	0.24	0.020	0.58	8.93
60	0.29	0.024	0.70	10.73
70	0.34	0.028	0.81	12.5
80	0.38	0.033	0.93	13.7
90	0.44	0.037	1.04	16.13
100	0.48	0.041	1.16	17.9
110	0.53	0.045	1.3	19.7
120	0.58	0.048	1.4	21.5
130	0.63	0.053	1.53	21.93
140	0.68	0.058	1.64	25.0
150	0.72	0.06	1.76	26.9
160	0.77	0.065	1.9	28.6
170	0.82	0.07	2.0	30.42
180	0.83	0.077	2.11	32.19
190	0.92	0.078	2.22	34.0
200	0.98	0.08	2.3	35.8
210	1.02	0.086	2.48	37.59
220	1.04	0.088	2.58	39.27
230	1.12	0.094	2.67	41.17
240	1.16	0.097	2.81	42.99

- (1) ONCE, BEFORE YOU ENTER AN AREA WHERE YOU ARE AT A HEIGHTENED RISK OF EXPOSURE TO THE ABOVE MICROBES, AND ONCE AFTER YOU HAVE LEFT THAT AREA, IF LESS THAN 16 HOURS SINCE EXPOSURE.
- (2) IF YOU HAVE BEEN EXPOSED TO THE ABOVE MICROBES: TWICE DAILY FOR TEN DAYS FOR PLAGUE, CHOLERA, AND TYPHOID FEVER. TWICE DAILY FOR TEN DAYS FOR ANTHRAX, THEN 1/2 INDICATED DOSAGE FOR AN ADDITIONAL 20 DAYS, THEN 1/4 OF INDICATED DOSAGE FOR 30 MORE DAYS.
- (3) FOUR TIMES DAILY FOR TEN DAYS -- AGGRESSIVE TREATMENT OF SEVERELY ILL PATIENTS

Take the 118A7 capsule filling machine Insert the 117A8 00 Empty Capsules and fill with the Terramycin powder. Each **LEVEL TEA SPOON = 6 CAPSULES**

An alternative would be to weigh out the terramycin powder and mix with a small amount of water, (about enough for a swallow), and chase with a glass of water. For children you can take a small glass of water, add the terramycin and a teaspoon of brown sugar. If the children object to the taste terramycin can also be mixed with a glass of CLUB SODA brought to room temperature, and swallowed swiftly. If a person starts hearing a ringing sound in the ears decrease dosage. (You will thank your lucky stars that you purchased the capsule machine and capsules so that this method could be avoided)

13 - 13 Oxy-Tet 100 Oxytetracycline HCl Injection (in povidone) (100mg. of oxytetracycline base as oxytetracycline HCl per ml.) may be obtained in quantities from farmers supply facilities (Quality Farm and Fleet, CO OP, LANDMARK, etc.). A warning on the label states for animal use only, however this product is identical to that used in hospitals and doctors offices. When properly used in the treatment of disease caused by Anthrax, Plague, Mycoplasma fermentans (incognitus) and secondary infections caused by microorganisms susceptible to Oxytetracycline HCl, most sick individuals that have been treated with these antibiotics show a noticeable improvement within 36 to 48 hours. Oxy-Tet 100 comes in a 500 ml (1.05 pint) multiple dosage sterile vial. This product is ready for immediate injection (**for intramuscular injection only**). Injection is made deep into the buttock muscle. The preferred sites are the upper outer quadrant of the buttock, i.e. gluteus maximus, (see illustration on page 83), and the mid-lateral thigh. CHILDREN: It is recommended that intramuscular injection be given in the mid-lateral muscles of the thigh. In infants and small children the periphery of the upper outer quadrant of the gluteal region should be used only when necessary, in order to minimize the possibility of damage to the sciatic nerve. Make sure the needle is not in a blood vessel: (After the needle is inserted, pull out slightly on the plunger, if blood comes into the syringe, reposition the needle). Before the injection, wash the injection site thoroughly with soap and water and then paint it with a germicide such as iodine or alcohol. Change the site for each subsequent injection. Rarely do side reactions or so-called allergic manifestations occur in individuals treated with this antibiotic. If any undesirable reactions are noted, discontinue the use of this drug immediately.

13 - 14 Oxy-Tet 100 Oxytetracycline HCl Dosage

- (1) ONCE, BEFORE YOU ENTER AN AREA WHERE YOU ARE AT A HEIGHTENED RISK OF EXPOSURE TO THE ABOVE MICROBES, AND ONCE AFTER YOU HAVE LEFT THAT AREA, IF LESS THAN 16 HOURS SINCE EXPOSURE.
- (2) IF YOU HAVE BEEN EXPOSED TO THE ABOVE MICROBES: TWICE DAILY FOR TEN DAYS FOR PLAGUE, CHOLERA, AND TYPHOID FEVER. TWICE DAILY FOR TEN DAYS FOR ANTHRAX, THEN 1/2 INDICATED DOSAGE FOR AN ADDITIONAL 20 DAYS, THEN 1/4 OF INDICATED DOSAGE FOR 30 MORE DAYS.
- (3) FOUR TIMES DAILY FOR TEN DAYS -- AGGRESSIVE TREATMENT OF SEVERELY ILL PATIENTS

DOSAGE DETERMINED BY BODY WEIGHT, REFER TO THE FOLLOWING CHART

POUNDS OF BODY WEIGHT	CUBIC CENTIMETERS OR MILLILITERS
0 TO 10	0.25
10 TO 40	1.0
40 TO 100	1.5 TO 2.5
100 TO 200	2.5 TO 4.0
200 OR OVER	4.0 TO 5.0

At the same agriculture store you purchased the Oxy-Tet 100 you also need to purchase hypodermic syringes and needles. These are usually kept under the counter or in a locked cabinet, and some places require you to sign for them, (do not be afraid of signing for the hypodermic syringe's or needles, however it is best to buy your entire supply at one time than over a period of time for they might think you are a junky). Purchase at least one vial of Oxy-Tet 100, preferably two, per family member under 100 lb. These have a very good shelf life, 2 or 3 years at room temperature, 5 years+ if kept in the refrigerator.

For every family member under 100 lb. purchase 20 B-D 5cc syringe with luer lok, part # 309603, and purchase # 40 B-D 21G 1- 1/4 PrecisionGuide Needles, part # 5166.

For every family member over 100 lb. purchase 2 vials of Agri-strep, preferably 3. For every family member over 100 lb. purchase ten 10 cc syringes with lur lok, and #20 B-D 21G 1-1/4 PrecisionGuide Needles, part # 5166.

You should have on hand three glass reusable hypodermic 10 cc syringes and three stainless steel reusable hypodermic needles 20G x 3/4, The needles can be purchased at the same agriculture store where you purchased the Oxy-Tet 100. However one may have to ask his friendly veterinary to obtain the glass hypodermic syringe, (some old vets have them laying around and will give them to you). These can be sterilized after each use in a home pressure cooker. Simply wrap individually each glass syringe and needle with aluminum foil. Place one cup of water in bottom of pressure cooker place rack in pressure cooker and place syringes and needles on rack. Pressure cook for at least 15 minutes after steam starts to escape. Leave syringes and needles wrapped until just before use. The Needles can be sharpened with a finger nail file before pressure cooking.

Giving The Injection
(Intramuscular, BUTTOCK, Injection only)

1. If the Oxy-Tet 100 has been kept in a refrigerator warm it to at least room temperature if time permits. Shake the Oxy-Tet 100 vial several times to thoroughly mix the antibiotics.
2. The top of the Oxy-Tet 100 vial has a rubber septum covered with a metal disk. Remove the disk. Clean the Oxy-Tet 100 rubber septum with alcohol.
3. If you are using a plastic dispersible syringe remove the wrapper, (if using glass remove aluminum foil). Get a hypodermic needle and remove wrapper, (if using reusable remove foil). Thread the needle onto the syringe after removing the plastic cap.
4. Take the vile of Oxy-Tet 100 in one hand and the hypodermic syringe and needle in the other hand. Push the needle through the septum in the top of the vile, invert the vile and start withdrawing the syringe plunger, withdraw until slightly more than called for on the above dosage chart, then withdraw the needle from the vial septum
5. If supplies of needles permit, and you are using dispersible needles, remove the needle from the syringe and install a new needle (the first needle was dulled when it was inserted in the vial septum). The reusable stainless steel needles are stronger and do not dull as quickly.
6. With the needle pointing up expel a small amount of the Oxy-Tet 100 making sure all air bubbles have been removed, (if there are several small air bubbles in the syringe try flicking the syringe with your finger to get the small bubbles to form one then expel it).

7. With the patient laying down, expose the buttock. The preferred sites are the upper outer quadrant of the buttock, i.e. gluteus maximus, (see illustration on page 83), and the mid-lateral thigh. CHILDREN: It is recommended that intramuscular injection be given in the mid-lateral muscles of the thigh. In infants and small children the periphery of the upper outer quadrant of the gluteal region should be used only when necessary, in order to minimize the possibility of damage to the sciatic nerve. With a cotton ball saturated with alcohol start rubbing the skin in a small circular pattern approximately one inch in diameter, for a full two minutes.

8. Smartly insert the needle into the circular pattern you have cleaned at approximately 45 degree angle to almost the full length of the needle, (a little less in young children).

9. Pull back slightly on the syringe plunger and notice if any blood appears in the syringe, if it does you have hit a vein and will have to reposition the needle in a slightly different position.

10. Push slowly but firmly on the syringe plunger, it will feel stiff but this is normal, until the entire contents of the syringe have been injected.

11. Withdraw the needle smartly.

12. Take an alcohol saturated swab and hold on the injection spot for two full minutes.

13. If you are using disposable syringes and needles, do not try to re-shield the used needle, dispose of properly (so that children will not get hold of it). If you are using reusable glass syringe and reusable stainless steel needles, wash thoroughly with hot water, then wrap in aluminum foil and sterilize in a pressure cooker before reuse.

13 - 15 Pen-Aqueous (Penicillin G Procane), Or Agri-Strept (Sterile Penicillin G Procaine And Dihydrostreptomycin Sulfate) may be obtained in quantities from farmers supply facilities (Quality Farm and Fleet, CO OP, LANDMARK, etc.). A warning on the label states for animal use only, however this product is identical to that used in hospitals and doctors offices. When properly used in the treatment of disease caused by Anthrax, Streptococcus pneumonia, and secondary infections caused by microorganisms susceptible to Penicillin or Dihydrostreptomycin, most individuals that have been treated with these antibiotics show a noticeable improvement within 36 to 48 hours. Agri-strep comes in a 100 ml multiple dosage sterile vial. This product is ready for immediate injection **(for intramuscular injection only)** after the vial is shaken to insure a uniform suspension. Injection is made deep into the buttock muscle, after making sure the needle is not in a blood vessel. (after the needle is inserted, pull out slightly on the syringe, if blood comes into the syringe, reposition the needle). The preferred sites are the upper outer quadrant of the buttock, i.e. gluteus maximus, (see illustration on page 83), and the mid-lateral thigh. CHILDREN: It is recommended that intramuscular injection be given in the mid-lateral muscles of the thigh. In infants and small children the periphery of the upper outer quadrant of the gluteal region should be used only when necessary, in order to minimize the possibility of damage to the sciatic nerve. Before the injection, wash the injection site thoroughly with soap and water and then paint it with a germicide such as iodine or alcohol. Change the site for each subsequent injection. Rarely do side reactions or so-called allergic manifestations occur in individuals treated with this antibiotic. If any undesirable reactions are noted, discontinue the use of this drug immediately.

13 - 16 AGRI-STREPT OR PEN-AQUEOUS DOSAGE

- (1) ONCE, BEFORE YOU ENTER AN AREA WHERE YOU ARE AT A HEIGHTENED RISK OF EXPOSURE TO ANTHRAX, AND ONCE AFTER YOU HAVE LEFT THAT AREA, IF LESS THAN 16 HOURS SINCE EXPOSURE.
- (2) IF YOU HAVE BEEN EXPOSED TO ANTHRAX: TWICE DAILY FOR TEN DAYS, THEN 1/2 INDICATED DOSAGE FOR AN ADDITIONAL 20 DAYS, THEN 1/4 OF INDICATED DOSAGE FOR 30 MORE DAYS.
- (3) FOUR TIMES DAILY FOR TEN DAYS -- AGGRESSIVE TREATMENT OF SEVERELY ILL PATIENTS. MAY ALSO BE USED TO TREAT STREPTOCOCCUS PNEUMONIA AND PULMONARY INFECTIONS.

DOSAGE DETERMINED BY BODY WEIGHT, REFER TO THE FOLLOWING CHART

POUNDS OF BODY WEIGHT	CUBIC CENTIMETERS OR MILLILITERS
0 TO 10	1.0
10 TO 40	2.0
40 TO 100	2.0 TO 5.0
100 TO 200	5.0 TO 8.0
200 OR OVER	8.0 TO 10.0

At the same agriculture store you purchased the AGRI-STREPT you also need to purchase hypodermic syringes and needles. These are usually kept under the counter or in a locked cabinet, and some places require you to sign for them, (do not be afraid of signing for the hypodermic syringe's or needles, however it is best to buy your entire supply at one time than over a period of time for they might think you are a junky). Purchase at least one vial of AGRI-STREPT, preferably two, per family member under 100 lb. These have a very good shelf life, 2 or 3 years at room temperature, 5 years+ if kept in the refrigerator.

For every family member under 100 lb. purchase 20 B-D 5cc syringe with luer lok, part # 309603, and purchase # 40 B-D 21G 1- 1/4 PrecisionGuide Needles, part # 5166.

For every family member over 100 lb. purchase 2 vials of Agri-strep, preferably 3. For every family member over 100 lb. purchase ten 10 cc syringes with lur lok, and #20 B-D 21G 1-1/4 PrecisionGuide Needles, part # 5166.

You should have on hand three glass reusable hypodermic 10 cc syringes and three stainless steel reusable hypodermic needles 20G x 3/4, The needles can be purchased at the same agriculture store where you purchased the AGRI-STREPT. However one may have to ask his friendly veterinary to obtain the glass hypodermic syringe, (some old vets have them laying around and will give them to you). These can be sterilized after each use in a home pressure cooker. Simply wrap individually each glass syringe and needle with aluminum foil. Place one cup of water in bottom of pressure cooker place rack in pressure cooker and place syringes and needles on rack. Pressure cook for at least 15 minutes after steam starts to escape. Leave syringes and needles wrapped until just before use. The Needles can be sharpened with a finger nail file before pressure cooking.

Giving The Injection
(Intramuscular, BUTTOCK, Injection only)

1. If the AGRI-STREPT OR PEN-AQUEOUS has been kept in a refrigerator warm it to at least room temperature if time permits. Shake the AGRI-STREPT OR PEN-AQUEOUS vial several times to thoroughly mix the antibiotics.
2. The top of the AGRI-STREPT OR PEN-AQUEOUS vial has a rubber septum covered with a metal disk. Remove the disk. Clean the rubber septum with alcohol.
3. If you are using a plastic dispersible syringe remove the wrapper, (if using glass remove aluminum foil). Get a hypodermic needle and remove wrapper, (if using reusable remove foil). Thread the needle onto the syringe after removing the plastic cap.
4. Take the vile of AGRI-STREPT OR PEN-AQUEOUS in one hand and the hypodermic syringe and needle in the other hand. Push the needle through the septum in the top of the vile, invert the vile and start withdrawing the syringe plunger, withdraw until slightly more than called for on the above dosage chart, then withdraw the needle from the vial septum
5. If supplies of needles permit, and you are using dispersible needles, remove the needle from the syringe and install a new needle (the first needle was dulled when it was inserted in the vial septum). The reusable stainless steel needles are stronger and do not dull as quickly.
6. With the needle pointing up expel a small amount of the AGRI-STREPT OR PEN-AQUEOUS making sure all air bubbles have been removed, (if there are several small air bubbles in the syringe try flicking the syringe with your finger to get the small bubbles to form one then expel it).
7. With the patient laying down, expose the buttock. The preferred sites are the upper outer quadrant of the buttock, i.e. gluteus maximus, (see illustration on page 83), and the mid-lateral thigh. CHILDREN: It is recommended that intramuscular injection be given in the mid-lateral muscles of the thigh. In infants and small children the periphery of the upper outer quadrant of the gluteal region should be used only when necessary, in order to minimize the possibility of damage to the sciatic nerve. With a cotton ball saturated with alcohol start rubbing the skin in a small circular pattern approximately one inch in diameter, for a full two minutes.
8. Smartly insert the needle into the circular pattern you have cleaned at approximately 45 degree angle to almost the full length of the needle, (a little less in young children).
9. Pull back slightly on the syringe plunger and notice if any blood appears in the syringe, if it does you have hit a vein and will have to reposition the needle in a slightly different position.
10. Push slowly but firmly on the syringe plunger, it will feel stiff but this is normal, until the entire contents of the syringe have been injected.
11. Withdraw the needle smartly.
12. Take an alcohol saturated swab and hold on the injection spot for two full minutes.
13. If you are using disposable syringes and needles, do not try to re-shield the used needle, dispose of properly (so that children will not get hold of it). If you are using reusable glass syringe and reusable stainless steel needles! Wash thoroughly with hot water, then wrap in aluminum foil and sterilize in a pressure cooker before reuse.

BACTERIOLOGICAL WARFARE

*The gluteal muscles are generally used for intramuscular injections (IM). When using this site you must be careful to avoid injuring the large nerves and blood vessels located in this area. The **fleshiest portion of the buttocks is <u>not</u> the safest for injections** because the sciatic nerve and the superior gluteal artery lie underneath. Injections in this area can cause severe pain and even paralyze the lower extremity when these structures are damaged.

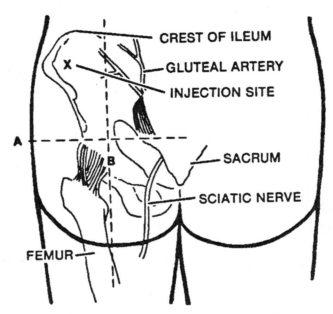

Administering intramuscular injection (gluteal muscles).

To locate a safe area for injection divide the buttocks into fourths, or quadrants. Palpate the ridge of the ilium and draw an imaginary line down to the lower edge of the buttocks. Draw a horizontal line from the upper edge of the acetabulum over to the spine and use the upper outer quadrant for intramuscular injection.

* Page 18-35 FM 8-230 Field Manual **Medical Specialist**, Headquarters Department of the Army, Washington, D.C.

BIOLOGICAL WARFARE

CHAPTER 14

TREATMENT FOR BIOLOGICAL AGENT CASUALTIES

14 - 1 Essentials Of Universal Safety Precautions For Health Care Providers.
1. Use appropriate barrier precautions to prevent skin and mucous membranes exposure, including wearing gloves at all times -- and masks, goggles, gowns, or aprons if there is a risk of splashes or droplet formation.
2. Thoroughly wash hands and other skin surfaces after gloves are removed and immediately after any contamination.
3. Take special care to avoid injuries with sharp objects such as needles and scalpels.
4. Use mouthpieces or other ventilation devices with one-way valves for performing any resuscitation measures.
5. If health-care workers have exuditive lesions or weeping dermatitis refrain from handling patient care equipment or patients
6. Through decontamination of any equipment that has been contaminated with any blood or body fluid before it is repaired or transported.
7. Very stringent adherence to precautions by pregnant workers.

These four microorganisms, in this order, are the most likely candidates for use in biological attack by a terrorist organization or nation. Therefore, these are the ones that we will concentrate our defense and treatment against.
► 1. YERSINIA PESTIS (PLAGUE),
► 2. BACILLUS ANTHRACIS (ANTHRAX)
► 3.VIBRIO CHOLERA (CHOLERA)
► 4. SALMONELLA TYPHI (TYPHOID FEVER).

If you've ever had the flu, you will remember that you were not sure just when or where you were exposed to the disease. Several days after you were exposed you began to feel sick. Diseases caused by biological agents appear in much the same way - a few days to weeks after contact with the agent.

14 - 2 FIRST AID FOR BIOLOGICAL AGENT CASUALTIES
If you suspect you have been exposed to a biological agent, thoroughly scrub your face and hands as soon as the situation permits. Use plenty of soap (a strong germicidal soap); brush your teeth and gums and then gargle with a hydrogen peroxide solution made from one ounce of 3% hydrogen peroxide and two ounces pure water. As soon as the situation permits, take a complete shower, using plenty of warm water and soap. If contaminated, all clothing should be decontaminated at the first opportunity.
If you suspect that a biological attack has been made, you must be doubly careful of what you eat and drink. Food and water are the natural homes of many disease producers; **eating contaminated food or drinking contaminated water is a sure way of getting biological agents into your body.** If biological agent contamination is **strongly suspected,** and you were wearing your respirator (GAS MASK) **you must at once decontaminate the outside**

of your body by taking a complete shower using plenty of warm water and soap. If clothing is contaminated, all of it should be decontaminated at the first opportunity. **Take The Appropriate Antibiotic Dosage For Your Body Weight Once, After You Have Left That Area Where You Were At A Heightened Risk Of Exposure To The Above Microbes, And Once More 12 Hours Later.**

If you were not wearing your respirator (GAS MASK) and/or you have eaten contaminated food or have been drinking contaminated water, take a complete shower using plenty of warm water and soap. If contaminated, all clothing should be decontaminated at the first opportunity. **You Must At Once Decontaminate The Inside Of The Body As Well By Taking The Appropriate Antibiotic Dosage For Your Body Weight Twice Daily For Six Days If You Have Been Exposed To Above Microbes**

14 - 3 First Aid For Yersinia Pestis (Plague)

Remember that untreated pneumonic plague kills from 98 to 100 percent of its victims, and that untreated intestinal plague kills 99.99 percent of its victims. Once pneumonic or intestinal plague is established, even with aggressive antibiotic therapy, it kills 95% of its victims.

If You Are Sure That You **Only Inhaled** The Plague Microbes And The Only Microbes That Got Into Your Intestinal System **Are Those That You Inhaled And Swallowed,** Take The Appropriate Antibiotic Dosage For Your Body Weight, Twice Daily For Ten Days,

If You Have Eaten Food Or Drank Water That You "Strongly" Suspect May Have Been Contaminated With Plague And More Than 12 Hours Has Elapsed Since Exposure, Take The Appropriate Antibiotic Dosage For Your Body Weight, Three Times Daily For Ten Days.

14 - 4 First Aid For Bacillus Anthracis (Anthrax)

Remember that untreated pneumonic anthrax kills from 98 to 100 percent of its victims, and that untreated intestinal anthrax kills 99.99 percent of its victims. Once pneumonic or intestinal anthrax is established, even with aggressive antibiotic therapy, it kills 95% of its victims. Assume that the microorganisms have contaminated the patients lungs, and if contaminated food or water have been consumed, Intestinal tract as well. The following decontamination procedure **must be taken at once.**

If You Are Sure That You **Only Inhaled** The Anthrax Microbes And The Only Microbes That Got Into Your Intestinal System Are Those That You Inhaled And Swallowed, And Less Than Six Hours Has Elapsed, Take The Appropriate Antibiotic Dosage For Your Body Weight, **Twice Daily For Six Days**, If More Than Six Hours Has Elapsed, Take The Appropriate Antibiotic For Your Body Weight, **Twice Daily For Ten Days, Then 1/2 Indicated Dosage For An Additional 20 Days, Then 1/4 Of Indicated Dosage For 30 More Days**

If You Have Ingested Food Or Water That You "Strongly" Suspect May Have Been Contaminated With Anthrax Microbes And Less Than 6 Hours Has Elapsed Since Exposure, Take The Appropriate Antibiotic Dosage For Your Body Weight, Three Times Daily For Ten Days. **If More Than 6 Hours Has Elapsed Since Exposure, Four Times Daily For Ten Days, Then 1/2 Indicated Dosage For An Additional 20 Days, Then 1/4 Of Indicated Dosage For 30 More Days**

14 - 5 First Aid For Vibrio Cholera (Cholera)

Remember that untreated cholera kills from 45 to 55 percent of its victims. Assume that the microorganisms have contaminated the intestinal tract and the following decontamination procedure must be taken at once.

If You Have Ingested Food Or Water That You "Strongly" Suspect May Have Been Contaminated With Cholera Microbes And Less Than 6 Hours Has Elapsed Since Exposure, Take The Appropriate Antibiotic Dosage For Your Body Weight, Two Times Daily = For Six Days. If More Than 6 Hours Has Elapsed Since Exposure, Three Times Daily = For Ten Days.

If You Come Down With Cholera, Use The Calf Electrolyte Formula Mixed In Water At A Rate Of 1 Quart Per 80 Pounds Of Body Weight 3-4 Times Per Day For 2 Days. For The Following 2 Days The Solution Should Be Diluted 1:1 With Milk.

14 - 6 First Aid For Salmonella Typhi (Typhoid Fever)

Remember that untreated Typhoid fever kills from 5 to 10 percent of its victims.

If You Only Suspect That You Have Ingested Water Or Food Contaminated With Salmonella Typhi And Less Than 6 Hours Has Elapsed Since Exposure, Take The Appropriate Antibiotic Dosage For Your Body Weight, Two Times Daily = For Four Days. If More Than 6 Hours Has Elapsed Since Exposure, Three Times Daily = For Six Days.

CHAPTER 15

TREATMENT

If A North American Citizen Gets A Disease From A Biological Agent, In Spite Of The Preventive Measures Taken, The Following Procedures Should Be Followed.

Essentials Of Universal Safety Precautions For Health Care Providers.
1. Use of appropriate barrier precautions to prevent skin and mucous membranes exposure, including wearing gloves at all times and masks, goggles, gowns, or aprons if there is a risk of splashes or droplet formation.
2. Thorough washing of hands and other skin surfaces after gloves are removed and immediately after any contamination.
3. Taking special care to avoid injuries with sharp objects such as needles and scalpels.
4. Use of mouthpieces or other ventilation devices with one-way valves for performing any resuscitation measures.
5. Refraining from handling patient care equipment or patients if health-care workers have exudative leasions or weeping dermatitis.
6. Very stringent adherence to precautions by pregnant workers.
7. Thorough decontamination of any equipment that has been contaminated with any blood or body fluid before it is repaired or transported.

15 - 1 Yersinia Pestis (Plague)
Sylvatic Plague (Spread By Infected Flea's, Bed Bugs, Lice)
Once in humans, cells of Y. pestis usually travel to the lymph nodes, where they cause the formation of swollen areas referred to as *buboes,* for this reason the disease is frequently referred to as bubonic plague. The buboes become filled with Y. pestis, but the distinct capsule on cells of Y pestis prevent them from being phagocytized. Secondary buboes form in peripheral lymph nodes and cells eventually enter the bloodstream, causing generalized septicemia. Multiple hemorrhages produce dark splotches on the skin. If not treated prior to the bacteremic stage, the symptoms of plague, including extreme lymph node pain, prostration, shock, and delirium, usually cause death within 3 to 5 days.
   TREATMENT
1. STRICT BED REST, keep the patient warm.
2. If the patient was bitten on the legs a bubo will usually form in the groin, with the patient laying on their back look for a raised area usually one to one and one half inch and usually 3 inches left or right of the reproductive organs (penis/vagina). The patient will be experiencing extreme pain in this area.
3. If the patient was bitten on the fingers or hands the bubo will form in the arm pit. With the patient laying on their back look for a one to one and one half inch raised area. The patient will be experiencing extreme pain in this area.
4. If the disease has progressed to this stage, the bubo must be aspirated!
   MEDICAL SUPPLIES NEEDED
✓   (a) One glass or plastic hypodermic syringe & needles.

✓ (b) Bottle of strong antiseptic (Iodine or alcohol).
✓ (c) Cotton ball or small piece of clean cloth.
✓ (d) Latex exam gloves.
PROCEDURE
1. First, put on a pair of latex exam gloves.
2. Next, thoroughly clean the surface of the bubo with a strong antiseptic.
3. Take the hypodermic needle & syringe and insert the needle into the top of the bubo, pulling back on the syringes plunger as you do. (If you are using a 3/4 needle you should not go in too deep.) This will reduce the pressure in the bubo and also reduce the pain, in addition this could prevent the bacteria from entering the blood stream. This aspirated material is highly infectious, treat it accordingly. Dispose of material to be removed from a glass hypodermic syringe by slowly injecting the aspirated material into a container of house hold bleach. Plastic disposable hypodermic syringe and needle should be incinerated.
4. <u>Start aggressive treatment with Terramycin or Panmycin.</u>

Pneumonic Plague

This occurs when cells of Y. pestis are either inhaled directly or reach the lungs during bubonic plague. Symptoms are usually absent until the last day or two of the disease when large amounts of bloody sputum are emitted. Untreated cases rarely survive more than 2 days. <u>Pneumonic plague, as one might expect, is a highly contagious disease, and can spread rapidly via the respiratory route if infected individuals are not immediately quarantined.</u>
TREATMENT
1. Immediately quarantined.
2. Put on your respirator , at once.
3. Put a surgical mask on the patient,(to help prevent spread of microbes).
4. <u>Start aggressive treatment with terramycin or panmycin.</u>

Septicemic Plague

This involves the rapid spread of Y. pestis throughout the body without the formation of buboes, and usually causes death before a diagnosis can be made.

15 - 2 Bacillus Anthracis (Anthrax)
Disease Produced

Anthrax may appear in three forms in man -- cutaneous, pulmonary, and intestinal. The cutaneous or skin form is characterized by carbuncles (boils) and swelling at the site of infection. Sometimes this local infection will develop into systemic infection. The pulmonary form, is an infection of the lungs contracted by inhalation of the spores. The intestinal form is contracted by eating contaminated food or insufficiently cooked meat of infected animals.
Cutaneous Anthrax (malignant pustule)

The mortality of untreated cutaneous anthrax ranges up to 25% and is most commonly found in individuals who have been exposed to a biological attack and who were wearing their respirator <u>but were not wearing an adequate protective garment, (tyvek sack suit).</u> Infection is initiated by the entrance of bacilli through an abrasion of the skin. A pustule usually appears on the hands or forearms. The bacilli are readily recognized under a microscope from the serosanguineous discharge.

TREATMENT
1. STRICT BED REST, keep the patient warm.
2. Aggressive treatment with Agri-Strept, (penicillin is the drug of choice for treatment). TERRAMYCIN OR PANMYCIN May be used with people who are allergic to penicillin.

MEDICAL SUPPLIES NEEDED
√ (1) One vial of agri-strept per patient.
√ (2) Glass reusable hypodermic syringe & needles or plastic disposable hypodermic syringes & needles.
√ (3) One bottle strong antiseptic.
√ (4) Cotton balls.
√ (5) Latex exam gloves.

Pulmonary Anthrax
1. The mortality rate in untreated pulmonary anthrax is almost 100%. This is the primary form of the disease found in individuals who were not wearing their respirator during an biological attack and breathed in the spores. The bacilli may be found in large numbers in the sputum if viewed under a microscope. If not properly treated, this form progresses to fatal septicemia.

TREATMENT
1. STRICT BED REST, keep the patient warm.
2. Aggressive treatment with Agri-Strept, (penicillin is the drug of choice for treatment).

Gastrointestinal Anthrax
The mortality rate in untreated gastrointestinal anthrax is 100%. This is the most severe form of anthrax. The bacilli or spores are swallowed, thus initiating intestinal infection. The organisms may be isolated from the patient's stools.

TREATMENT
1. STRICT BED REST, keep the patient warm.
2. Aggressive treatment with Agri-Strept, (penicillin is the drug of choice for treatment).

15 - 3 Vibro Cholera (Cholera)
Disease Produced
Cholera, an acute infectious gastrointestinal disease, is characterized by sudden onset with nausea, vomiting, profuse watery diarrhea with "rice-water" appearance, rapid loss of body fluids, toxemia, and frequent collapse. The mortality rate in untreated cholera is almost 50%. This is the primary form of the disease found in individuals who were not wearing their respirator during an biological attack and breathed in and swallowed the microorganisms, or who drank contaminated water or ate contaminated food.

MEDICAL MATERIALS NEEDED
√ (1) Minimum of 30 packs of ANCHOR ORAL REHYDRATION ,Calf Rehydration Powder per person. Or 30 packs of BIOLYTE Calf Electrolyte Formula.
√ (2) One quart container.

BACTERIOLOGICAL WARFARE

TREATMENT

The first consideration, in the treatment of cholera, is to replenish fluid and mineral losses of the body. This can be accomplished by taking either BIOLYTE or ANCHOR Calf rehydration powder and dissolving one package in one quart of known pure water (distilled or boiled water cooled to room temperature). Although the package says that it is not for human use it is in fact the same formula used in hospitals through out India. Administer the solution by feeding at the rate of 1 quart per 80 pounds body weight 3 to 4 times daily for 4 days as the only source of oral fluids. Drug therapy has little or no effect upon the clinical course of the disease. However, terramycin, given by mouth, causes rapid disappearance of the vibrio organisms, thus reducing the spread of the disease.

15 - 4 Salmonella Typhosa (Typhoid Fever)
Disease Produced

Typhoid fever is a systemic infection characterized by continued fever, lymphoid tissue involvement, ulceration of the intestines, enlargement of the spleen, rose-colored spots on the skin, diarrhea, and constitutional disturbances. The mortality in untreated cases range from 0 to 10 percent. This is the primary form of the disease found in individuals who were not wearing their respirator during an biological attack and breathed in and swallowed the microorganisms, or who drank contaminated water or ate contaminated food.

TREATMENT
1. Bed rest. Keep patient warm.
2. Give no solid food, and only broths, (ulceration of the intestines).
3. Salmonella infections are self-limiting and should not be treated with antibiotics as treatment may encourage development of carrier state. If treatment is warranted, ampicillin or trimethoprim-sulfamethoxazol is the drug of choice and should only be used for life-threatening illness.

CHAPTER 16

THE PROTECTIVE MASK
FM 21-41

16 - 1 Masking

Your Mask Is Your First Line Of Defense Against Biological Agents. Take Care Of It. Inhaling airborne microorganisms is the greatest danger in biological operations. A properly fitted protective mask, which has been kept in good condition, will completely protect you against inhaling microorganisms present in the air. Therefore, putting on your protective mask at the *first* indication or suspicion that the enemy is using a biological agent aerosol is just as important as masking at the first sign of a toxic chemical attack. Since you cannot detect the presence of biological agents, you must continue to wear your mask until you are instructed to remove it. Your community leaders will base decisions on information received from intelligence sources and on advice received from Offical sources.

16 - 2 Your Lifesaver

This chapter is written to help you perform your job under Chemical, Biological conditions and live to tell about it. While individual protection in chemical and biological operations is not the result of any single act, one idea should now be clear to you. Your protective mask is the number one item of protection against toxic chemicals and biological agents. Known in World Wars I and II simply as a gas mask, its value has increased *many* times. Today it is called a protective mask because it protects you against inhaling biological and chemical agents.

As you now know, survival in biological operations depends upon preventing biological agents from getting on or entering your body. While the protective mask alone cannot do this, it does play the major role. It prevents you from inhaling or from getting into your eyes all known biological agent aerosols. To say that your protective mask is a life saver is to state a true and simple fact.

16 - 3 How Protective Masks Work

A protective mask is a cover, or shield, against harmful substances in the air, just as a house is a shield against wind and rain. To protect you from breathing toxic substances, your mask contains a filter unit. This filter prevents toxic chemical agent vapors and toxic solid or liquid particles from reaching your face, eyes, and lungs. When you wear a mask, you draw air into it by inhaling. This air is purified by a filter unit before it enters your nose or mouth. There are two types of field protective masks that will be discussed here: The US Mask, protective M17 A1, which has two filter pads instead of a canister; the Draeger German gas mask, Russian gas mask, and Israeli gas mask, which has a canister.

16 - 4 The M17 Mask

The filter unit of the M17 mask consist of two filter pads contained in pouches molded in the cheek of the face piece. These filter pads, or filter elements, are both mechanical and chemical purifiers. Each filter element consist of two layers of mineral fiber and charcoal. Air is inhaled through two inlet valves, one located on the outer surface of each cheek pouch. The incoming filtered air passes from the cheek pouches through deflector tubes which direct the air across the lenses. The filtered air then passes through two one-way valves, one in each side of the nosecup. Breathing may be through either the nose or the mouth. Exhaled air is discharged through an outlet valve at the chin positions. The M17 mask assembly includes the mask, the carrier, and two lens outserts. The two lens outserts are provided for attachment over the mask lenses in much the same manner as storm windows are fitted over house windows. The outserts are used in very cold regions to prevent fogging of the lenses by condensation of exhaled breath. The outlet valve contains a voicemitter, which makes it possible to communicate understandably. Pockets designed to hold the protective mask waterproofing bag, as well as the lens outserts, are built into the M17 carrier. The M17 A1 mask has a drinking tube in the front of the mask and a small handle that can be used to bring the drinking straw to your mouth. There is also a canteen cap with a valve that will fit the standard military canteen, in addition to a rubber tube and valve insert on the front of the mask one can use to get a drink of water without having to take the mask off. Additional filter elements can also be obtained in addition to a hood, (field protective mask) to completely encapsulate your head.

The M17 A1 Mask Can Be Obtained From:

NITRO-PACK PREPAREDNESS CENTER 151 NORTH MAIN ST. HEBER CITY UTAH 84032   TEL# 310 802-0099   801 654-0099 800 866-4876
(1) M17 A1 protective mask $159.95
(2) FILTER ELEMENT SET (EXTRA) $18.95
(3) HOOD, FIELD PROTECTIVE MASK 4240-978-9432 $4.00

16 - 5 The Draeger German Gas Mask, Russian Gas Mask, Israeli Gas Mask

These are canister-type masks. (the inlet plug and closure cap must be removed and discarded for the canister to be effective.) As you inhale, the air first passes through the canister, which contains a purifying system consisting of a mechanical filter and a chemical filling. The mechanical filter clears the air by trapping tiny solid and liquid particles (in the form of aerosols). Then the chemical filling receives the air and absorbs (condenses and holds) the toxic vapors. Charcoal is used in the chemical filter, because it is a powerful absorbent. After the air is purified by the canister, it passes into your facepiece, where it is inhaled. Exhaled air is expelled from the facepiece through an outlet valve, which opens to allow this air to escape. The canister mask has two major parts: facepiece assembly, and canister.

The Draeger German Gas Mask, Israeli Gas Mask Can Be Obtained From:

NITRO-PACK PREPAREDNESS CENTER 151 NORTH MAIN ST. HEBER CITY UTAH 84032   TEL# 310 802-0099   801 654-0099 800 866-4876
(1) THE DRAGER PROTECTIVE MASK $34.95 (this mask can be worn for long periods of time).
(2) THE ISRAELI PROTECTIVE MASK $19.95 , SPARE FILTERS $8.99

The Russian Gas Mask, Israeli Gas Mask Can Be Obtained From:

THE SPORTSMAN GUIDE 411 FARWELL AVENUE SO. ST. PAUL, MN 55075-0239 TEL# 800-888-3006.
(1) THE RUSSIAN MASK $9.99 EXTRA FILTER $4.99
(2) THE ISRAELI MASK $9.99 EXTRA FILTER $4.99

16.6 Correct Fit And Adjustment Are Important

You know that toxic chemical agents, such as nerve gas are very deadly. Biological agents may be equally dangerous even though they do not cause immediate irritation and do not produce immediate symptoms. For you to stop breathing and to put on a mask upon suspicion of a biological agent aerosol is not enough to keep these agents out of your body. Your mask must fit your head and face so that it will be airtight when you have properly donned it. Many individuals make the mistake of pulling the straps too tight. Correct adjustment does not mean an extremely tight fit, but rather a close fit. Individuals with full beards may believe that they cannot get a good airtight seal unless they shave, this is a myth, in fact, individuals with full beards are able to obtain a better seal than those who shave. A fact that has been proven time and time again by the Russians.

Speed In Putting On Mask Versus An Airtight Seal

You may ask which is more important: speed in putting on the mask, or getting an airtight seal. Both are absolutely necessary. You must become expert both in putting on your mask and in getting an airtight seal in only a few seconds.

Tips On Donning Your Mask

You know that, in your everyday life, doing certain things in the same way every time saves you much time and effort. Donning your protective mask is no more complicated than putting on your hat, if you always go through the proper motions in the proper order.

1. In removing your mask from the carrier, always grasp it in the area of the nosecup, which is below the eyepieces. Remember that dirty hand prints on the eyepieces will interfere with your vision and will only have to be removed. Never remove the mask from the carrier by pulling on the outlet valve.

2. To put on your mask, grasp the facepiece with both hands and slide your thumbs inside so that the facepiece is opened to the fullest extent. Grasping the head harness tends to pull the edges to gather which makes it very difficult to get the mask over your face.

3. As you seat the chin pocket firmly and bring the head harness over your head, be sure that all head straps are straight and that the head pad is centered. Otherwise, the mask will be uncomfortable, and you may not get a seal around the facepiece. Head straps can best be adjusted by a quick jerk or pull, rather than a steady pull.

4. Use firm upward and outward strokes to smooth edges of the facepiece and press them to your face.

5. Always check your mask. To clear the M17 mask, place the palm of your right hand over the outlet valve opening with the forearm nearly parallel to the floor. Blow into the mask forcibly with the air that is already in your lungs. Air escapes around the facepiece, forcing the contaminated air out. Then, to test for leaks, place the palms of your hands over the two inlet valves in the cheek pouches and breath in slowly. The facepiece should collapse if the mask fits properly. Procedures for checking the canister-type mask are similar to those for the M17 mask, except that to clear the canister-type mask cup the palm of your right hand over the opening of the outlet valve, with the elbow pointing toward the ground. To test the canister-type mask, place your hand over the air inlet of the canister.

6. In removing your mask, follow the procedures for the type mask you are wearing. To remove the M17 mask, grasp faceplate by voicemitter-outlet valve assembly with the right hand. Remove the mask using a downward, outward, then upward motion. To

remove the canister-type mask unfasten the neck strap, grasp the mask in the nosecup area, and use the same circular motion (downward-outward-upward) as used in removing the M17 mask. Never remove the canister-type mask by grasping the outlet valve.

7. Take care to properly replace your mask in the carrier. This is well worth the few seconds it takes. The next time you have to take it out and put it on may be "for real." Make sure that the head harness is folded into the facepiece. Again, keep your hands off the eyepiece.

16 - 7 **Its Your Baby**

You are responsible for the care of your protective mask. In view of what you have learned about the great dangers of biological operations, it hardly seems necessary to explain in detail why you must take excellent care of your mask. (You should never carry the canister inside the facepiece of the canister-type mask.)

Water damages the filter elements of the M17 mask and the canister of the canister-type mask thereby destroying their efficiency. Use a waterproofing bag (small plastic garbage bag) during continued hard rain and at any time when water is likely to soak through the mask carrier. In a personal decontamination procedure, take a strong disinfectant placed on a cloth and go over the outside rubber areas of the mask. Remove your mask just before you step under the shower.

A protective mask is vital. Purchase the best one that you can afford, for your protective mask is vital to your safety when biological agent aerosols are used. Take care of it and it will take care of you.

CHAPTER 17

WATER

Bacillus Anthracis:
The spores are very stable and may remain alive for many years in water.
Vibrio Cholera:
The organism will survive up to 24 hours in sewage, and as long as 6 weeks in certain types of impure water containing salt and organic matter.
Yersinia Pestis (Plague):
The organism will remain viable in water from 2 to 30 days. At near freezing temperatures it will remain alive for months.
Salmonella typhosa:
The organism remains viable for 2 to 3 weeks in water, up to 3 months in ice and snow.

17 - 1 Water And Salt Requirements

In a well-organized terrorist attack this country's electric power grid would make a very tempting target especially in conjunction with wide spread germ attacks. By taking out only a small number of critical components (to which there are now no backups) electric power could be disrupted from weeks to months. In modern day North America 90% to 97% of modern homes depend on electricity for maintaining a constant supply of fresh water.

Painful thirst has been experienced by very few Americans. We take for granted that we will always have enough water to drink. Most of us think of "food and water" in that order when we think of survival essentials that should be stored. If unprepared citizens are confronted with a long term electrical power outage, they soon will realize that they should have given first priority to storing adequate water.

For the kidneys to eliminate waste products effectively, the average person needs to drink enough water so that he urinates at least one pint each day. (When water is not limited, most people drink enough to urinate 2 pints. Additional water is lost in perspiration, exhaled breath, and excrement.) Under cool conditions, a person could survive for weeks on 3 pints of water a day -- if he eats but little food and if that food is low in protein. Four to five quarts of drinking water per day are essential in very hot weather, with none allowed for washing. A minimum of 15 gallons per person should be stored. This amount usually will provide for some water remaining after two weeks to prevent thirst in case additional fresh water is still difficult to obtain.

When one is sweating heavily and not eating salty food, salt deficiency symptoms, especially cramping, are likely to develop within a few days. To prevent these, 6 or 8 grams of salt (about 1/4 ounce, or 1/2 tablespoon) should be consumed daily in food and drink. If little or no food is eaten, this small daily salt ration should be added to drinking water. Under hot conditions, a little salt makes water taste better.

17 - 2 Disinfecting Water

Boiling for 20 minutes is required to kill Plague, Cholera, and Typhoid microbes. Boiling for two **hours** is required to kill Anthrax spores.

Any household bleach that contains sodium hypochlorite as its only active ingredient, such as Clorox, may be used as a source of chlorine for disinfecting. The amount of sodium hypochlorite, usually 5.25%, is printed on the label. In recent years, perhaps as a precaution against drinking undiluted chlorine bleach solution, some household bleach containers show a warning such as "Not For Personal Use." This warning can be safely disregarded if the label states that the bleach contains only sodium hypochlorite as its active ingredient, and is used only in the small quantities specified in these and other instructions to disinfect water. Add 1 scant teaspoon per each 10 gallons of clear water and stir. Add 2 scant teaspoonfuls if the water is muddy or colored. Wait at least 30 minutes before drinking to allow enough time for the chlorine to kill all the microorganisms. Properly disinfected water should have a slight chlorine odor.

To disinfect small quantities of water, put 2 drops of household bleach containing 5.25 % sodium hypochlorite in each quart of clear water. Use 4 drops if the water is muddy or colored. If a dropper is not available, use a spoon and a square-ended strip of paper or thin cloth about 1/4 inch wide by 2 inches long. Put the strip in the spoon with an end hanging down about 1/2 inch beyond the end of the spoon. Then when bleach is placed in the spoon and the spoon is carefully tipped, drops in the size of those from a medicine dropper will drip off the end of the strip.

2% tincture of iodine can be used as a second choice. Add 5 drops to each quart of clear water and let stand 30 minutes. If the water is cloudy, add 10 drops to each quart. Commercial water purification tablets should be used as directed.

17 - 3 Sources Of Water

Other sources of drinking water should be located before the stored supply has been exhausted. The main water sources are given below, with the safest source listed first and the other sources listed in decreasing order of safety.

1. Water from deep wells and from water tanks and covered reservoirs into which no microbes have been introduced. (Caution: Although most spring water would be safe, some spring water is surface water that has flowed into and through underground channels without having been filtered.)
2. Water from covered seepage pits or shallow hand-dug wells. This water is safe IF germ-aerosols or germ contaminated surface water has been prevented from entering by waterproofing coverings and by waterproofing the surrounding ground to keep water from running down the outside well casing.
3. Contaminated water from deep lakes -- Water from a deep lake would be less contaminated by germ-aerosols than water from a shallow pond if both had the same area for deposits. Furthermore, germ-aerosols and germ spores settle to the bottom more rapidly in deep lakes than in shallow ponds. Water is agitated by the wind and in shallow ponds the disturbance reaches the bottom.
4. Contaminated water from shallow ponds and other shallow still water.
5. Contaminated water from streams, which would be especially dangerous if the stream is muddy from the first heavy rains after the germ attack. The first runoff will contain most of the germs that can be washed off the drainage area. Runoff after the first few heavy rains following the deposit of germ-aerosols is not likely to contain much deadly germs or germ spores.

6. Water collected from germ-aerosols contaminated roofs. This would contain more germs than would the runoff from the ground.

7. Water obtained by melting snow that has fallen through air containing germ aerosols, or snow lying on the ground onto which germ-aerosols has fallen. Avoid using such water for drinking or cooking, if possible.

17 - 4 Water From Wells

The wells of farms and rural homes would be the best sources of water for millions of survivors after a massive Germ Warfare attack. An attack in which the electrical power grid was also targeted by damaging power stations, transformers, and transmission lines would leave the electric pumps in those wells useless unless a source of emergency power was available. If electrical power is not available, the pump and its pipe could be removed from the well casing so that bail-cans could be used to reach the water and bring up enough for drinking and basic hygiene.

A very good bailer can be obtained for around $27 from Lehmans Hardware and Appliance. One Lehman Circle, PO Box 41 Kidron Ohio 44636 (USA) Phone 1-216-857-557. You should also obtain about 200 to 300 feet of good strong nylon rope. (Parachute cord is one of the lightest and strongest.)

CHAPTER 18

Food and Health

18 - 1 Food

The average American is accustomed to eating regularly and abundantly. They may not realize that for most people food would not be essential for survival during the first two or three weeks following a Germ Warfare attack. Exceptions are infants, small children, and the aged and sick, some of whom might die within a week without proper nourishment. Usually other things are more important for short-term survival: adequate shelter, adequate supply of breathable air, and enough water.

Most people do not realize that small daily amounts of a few unprocessed staple foods can enable them to survive for months, or even for years. A healthy person, if they are determined to live and if they learn to prepare and use whole-grain wheat or corn, can maintain their health for several months. If beans are available and are substituted for some of the grain, the ration will be improved and can maintain health for many months. The practical knowledge that will be given in this chapter about the expedient processing and cooking of basic grains and beans is based on old ways that are mostly unknown to modern Americans. The information contained in this chapter should enable you to live on the foods that most of the world's population consumes: grains, beans, and vegetables.

The nutritional information given in this chapter is taken from a July 1979 publication, *Maintaining Nutritional Adequacy During a Prolonged Food Crisis.*

18 - 2 Food For Home Occupants

The best way to assure you and your loved ones do not become infected after a massive Germ Warfare attack is to stay inside your home and not take any unnecessary trips outside.

Most people will need very little food to live several weeks. In most American homes there are only enough ready-to-eat, concentrated foods to last a few days. Obviously, it would be an important survival advantage to keep on hand a two-week supply of easily transportable foods. In any case, occupants of homes will be uncertain about when they can get more food and will have to make hard decisions about how much to eat each day.

When survivors of a germ attack leave their homes and start returning to work may mark the beginning of a much longer period of privation and hard work. A single massive multiple terrorist Germ Warfare attack on a large city could in 24 to 48 hours kill upwards of 2,000,000 individuals if Anthrax was used. It could take several weeks or months just to dispose of the corpses. During this period the possibility of dispersal of new Anthrax spores and reinfection will be high. The job you had in that city might not be there for months, if ever. Therefore, to maintain physical strength and morale, you ideally should have enough healthy food to provide well-balanced, adequate meals for many weeks.

During the first few weeks of a food crisis, lack of vitamins and other essentials of a well-balanced diet will not be of primary importance to previously well-nourished people. Healthful foods with enough calories to provide adequate energy will meet short-term needs. If water is in short supply, high-protein foods such as meat are best eaten only in moderation. A person eating high-protein foods requires more water than is needed when consuming an equal number of calories from foods high in carbohydrates.

18 - 3 Expedient Processing Of Grains And Soybeans

Whole-kernel grains or soybeans cannot be eaten in sufficient quantities to maintain vigor and health if merely boiled or parched. A little boiled whole-kernel wheat is a pleasant breakfast cereal, but people get sore tongues and very loose bowels when they try to eat enough boiled whole-kernel wheat to supply even half of their daily energy needs. Even the most primitive peoples grind or pound grains into meal or paste before cooking (Rice is the only important exception.) Few Americans know how to process whole-kernel grains and soybeans (our largest food reserves) into meal. This ignorance could be fatal to survivors of a Germ attack.

You need to obtain a grain mill. One of the finest compact & versatile grain mills we've tested, The Back To Basics grain mill, can be obtained for $64.95 from NITRO-PACK PREPAREDNESS CENTER 151 NORTH MAIN ST. HEBER CITY UTAH 84032 1-800-866-4876. It also can be obtained from Lehmans Hardware and Appliances One Lehman Circle, PO Box 41 Kidron, Ohio 44636 (USA) 1-216-857-5757, Fax 1-216-857-5785 Priced At $75.95. This is fine for wheat, but for corn you need a larger grain mill. One of the finest and fastest Hand Mills I have personally tested can also be obtained from Lehmans Hardware and Appliances. priced at $153.50 Catalogue #232. Another excellent Grain mills is the Catalogue # C-17A priced at $139.00 (also order # C-7B priced at $39.00 if you are going to grind oily material).

To lessen their laxative effects, all grains should be ground as fine as possible. Grains will be digested easier if they are finely ground.

18 - 4 Cooking With Minimum Fuel

In areas of heavy Terrorist Germ attacks, where terrorists have also targeted the electric power grid, you will have to remain **continuously** in your home for many days. Then you will have to stay in your home most of each 24 hours for weeks. You probably will soon consume all of your ready-to-eat foods. Therefore, unless you have the older type of gas stove that does not require electricity, you should have a portable, efficient cook stove. A cook stove is important for another reason: to help maintain morale. Even in warm weather you need some hot food and drink for comfort and to promote a sense of well-being. This is particularly true when you are under stress.

A kerosene cookstove fills this need nicely. Easily lighting with a match it is ready to use immediately, with no preheating hassles, with a hot blue flame and next-to-no-odor.

One of the finest compact, portable, and versatile Kerosene Cookstoves we've tested is The International Brand. It will run for 16 hours on one gallon of fuel, can be obtained from NITRO-PACK PREPAREDNESS CENTER 151 NORTH MAIN ST. HEBER CITY UTAH 84032 1-800-866-4876, and is priced at $74.95. Replacement wick is $7.95. Also can be obtained from Lehmans Hardware and Appliances One Lehman Circle, PO Box 41 Kidron, Ohio 44636 (USA) 1-216-857-5757, Fax 1-216-857-5785 Priced At $85.00. Catalogue # T-204 Replacement which-Last over a year! # RW-204; $7.95 This Kerosene Cookstove can also serve as a 8500 BTU heater.

BACTERIOLOGICAL WARFARE

In addition the kerosene cookstove you need to obtain at least 3 or 4 five gallon fuel cans, which can be picked up at many hardware stores, and fill them with kerosene. Kerosene will store virtually indefinitely.

18 - 5 Cooking Grain Alone

The best way to cook meal is first bring the water to a boil. Remove from the heat and quickly stir the meal into the hot water. Use 3 parts water to 1 part meal. Add 1 teaspoon (5 grams) of salt per pound of dry meal. (If the meal is stirred into briskly boiling water, lumping becomes a worse problem.) Then, while stirring constantly, again bring pot to a rolling boil. Since the meal is just beginning to swell, more unabsorbed water remains, so there is less sticking and scorching than if the meal were added to cold water and then brought to a boil. The hot cereal only has to be boiled and stirred long enough so that no thin, watery parts remain. This usually takes about 5 minutes. Continue to cook by boiling an additional 15 or 20 minutes.

When it is necessary to boil grain meal for many minutes, minimize sticking and scorching by cooking 1 part of dry meal with at least 4 parts of water. However, cooking a thinner hot cereal has a disadvantage during a food crisis. An increased volume of food must be eaten to satisfy one's energy needs.

If grain were the only food available, few Americans doing physical work could eat enough of it to maintain their weight at first, until their digestive tracts enlarged from eating very bulky foods. This adaption could take a few months. Small children could not adjust adequately to an all-grain diet; for them, concentrated foods such as fats also are needed to provide enough calories to maintain growth and health.

18 - 6 Cooking Grain And Beans Together

When soybeans are being used to supplement the lower quality proteins of grain, first grind the beans into a fine meal. To reduce cooking time further, soak the bean meal for a couple of hours keeping it covered with water as it swells. Next put the soaked bean meal into a pot containing about 3 times as much water as the total volume of the bean meal and the dry grain meal. Gently boil the bean meal for about 15 minutes, stirring frequently.

Stop boiling and add the grain meal while stirring constantly. Again bring the pot to a boil, stirring to prevent sticking and scorching, and boil until the meal has swelled enough to have absorbed all the water. After salting, boil the grain-bean mush for another 15 minutes or more before eating.

Whole soybeans must be boiled for a couple of hours to soften them sufficiently. Also, soybeans boiled alone have a taste that most people find objectionable. If soybeans are ground into a fine meal and then boiled with meal made from corn or another grain, they give a sweetish taste to the resulting mush. The unpleasant soybean taste is eliminated. If cooked as described above, soybeans and other beans or dried peas can be made digestible and palatable with minimum cooking.

18 - 7 100% Grain and 100% Bean Diets

A diet consisting solely of wheat, corn, or rice and salt has most of the essential nutrients. The critical deficiencies would be vitamins A, C, and D. Such a grain-based diet can serve adults and older children as their "staff of life" for months. Table 18.1 shows how less than 1 3/4 pounds of whole wheat or dry yellow corn satisfies most of the essential nutritional requirements

103

of a long-term emergency ration. Expedient ways of supplying the nutrients missing from these rations are described in a following section of this chapter.

Other common whole grains would serve about as well as wheat and yellow corn. At least 1/6 ounce of salt per day (about 5 grams) is essential for any ration that is to be eaten for more than a few days. 1/3 ounce (about 10 g or 3/4 tablespoon) should be available to allow for increased salt needs and to make grain and beans more palatable. This additional salt would be consumed as needed.

To repeat: few Americans at first would be able to eat the 3 or 4 quarts of thick mush that would be necessary with a ration consisting solely of whole-kernel wheat or corn. Only healthy Americans determined to survive would be likely to fare well for months on such unaccustomed and monotonous food as an all-grain diet. Eating two or more different kinds of grain and cooking in different ways would make an all-grain diet both more acceptable and more nourishing.

Not many people would be able to eat 27 ounces (dry weight before cooking) of beans in a day, and fewer yet could eat a daily ration of almost 23 ounces of soybeans. Beans as single-food diets are not recommended because their large protein content requires the drinking of more fluids. Roasted peanuts would provide a better single-food ration.

TABLE 18.1
Daily rations of 100% grain, beans, or peanuts (a)

	Wheat	Corn	Rations	Soybeans	Red Beans	Peanuts
Weight	790 g 27.8 OZ.	755 g 26.4 OZ.		645 g 22.7 OZ.	760 g 26.8 OZ.	447 g 15.8 OZ.
Energy, Kcal	2600	2600	2600	2600	2600	2600
Protein, g	103	67	55(c)	220	171	117
Fat, g	15	29	30	114	11	218
Calcium, mg	324	165	400	1458	836	322
Magnesium, mg	1260	1100	200-300	1710	1240	782
Iron, mg	26	15.7	10	54.2	52.4	9.8
Potassium, mg	2920	2130	1500-2000	10800	7420	3132
Vitamin A, RE	0	368	555	52	15	0
Thiamine, mg	4.3	2.8	1.0	7.1	3.9	1.3
Riboflavin, mg	1.0	0.9	1.4	2.0	1.5	1.3
Niacin, mg	34.0	16.5(d)	17.0	14.2	17.5	76.4
Vitamin C, mg	0	0	15-30	0	0	0
Vitamin D, ug	0	0	0(e)	0	0	0

► (a) Salt (1/3 ounce or 10 grams, or 3/4 tablespoon) should be available. This would be consumed as needed.

► (b) White corn supplies no Vitamin A, whereas yellow corn supplies 49 RE (retinol, a measure of Vitamin A Value) per 100 grams dry weight. Most corn in the United States is yellow corn.

► (c) If a diet contains some animal protein such as meat, eggs, or milk, the recommended protein would be less than 55 grams per day. If most of the protein is from milk or eggs, only 41 grams per day is recommended.

► (d) The niacin in corn is not fully available unless the corn is treated with an alkali, such as the lime or ashes Mexicans (and many Americans) add to the water in which corn kernels are soaked or boiled.

► (e) Although adults do not need vitamin D, infants, and pregnant or lactating women should receive 10 ug (10 micrograms).

► All grains are weighed dry.

18 - 8 GRAIN SUPPLEMENTED WITH BEANS

People who live on essentially vegetarian diets eat a little of their higher-quality protein food *at every meal,* along with the grain that is their main source of nutrition. Thus Mexicans eat some beans along with their corn tortillas, and Chinese eat a little fermented soybean food or a bit of meat or fish with a bowl of rice. Nutritionists have found that grains are low in some of the essential amino acids that the human body needs to build its proteins. For long-term good health, the essential amino acids must be supplied in the right proportions *with each meal* by eating some foods with more complete proteins than grain has. Therefore, in a prolonged food crisis one should strive to eat *at every meal* at least a little of any higher-quality protein foods that are available. These include ordinary beans, soybeans, milk powder, meat, and eggs.

Table 18.2 shows that by adding 7.0 ounces (200 grams) of red beans (or other common dried beans) to 2.1 ounces (600 grams) of either whole wheat or yellow corn, with salt added, you can produce rations that contain adequate amounts of all the important nutrients except vitamin A, vitamin C, vitamin D, and fat. If 5.3 ounces (150 grams) of soybeans are substituted for the red beans, the fat requirement is satisfied. The 600 grams of yellow corn contains enough carotene to enable the body to produce more than half the emergency recommendation of vitamin A. The small deficiencies in riboflavin would not cause sickness.

Other abundant grains, such as grain sorghums or barley, may be used instead of the wheat or corn shown in Table 18.2 to produce fairly well-balanced rations. Other legumes would serve to supplement grain about as well as red beans. (Peanuts are the exception: although higher in energy (fat) than any other unprocessed food, the quality of their protein is not as high as that of other legumes.)

Table 18.2
Daily rations of whole wheat or yellow corn supplemented with soybeans or red beans.
Recommended daily salt ration, including salt in food: 3/4 tablespoon (3/3 ounces or 10 grams).

A= 600g (21.1 oz.). Whole wheat plus 200g (7.0 oz.) Red Beans (dry weight).
B= 600g (21.1 oz.). Whole wheat plus 150g (5.3 oz.) Soybeans (dry weight).
C= Emergency recommendations
D= 600g (21.1 oz.) Yellow corn (a) plus 150g (5.3 oz.) soybeans (dry wt.).
E= 600g (21.1 oz.) Yellow corn plus 200g (7.0 oz.) Red beans (dry wt.).

	A	**B**	**C**	**D**	**E**
Energy, kcal	2,666	2,585	2,600	2,693	2,774
Protein	123	129	55(b)	105	98
Fat, g	15	39	30	50	26
Calcium, mg	466	585	400	471	352
Magnesium, mg	1,286	1,358	200-300	1,280	1.208
Iron, mg	33.6	32.4	10	25.2	26.4
Potassium, mg	4,188	4,736	1,500-2,000	4,220	3,672
Vitamin A, RE	4	12	555	306	298
Thiamine, mg	4.3	5.0	1.0	3.9	3.2
Riboflavin, mg	1.1	1.2	1.4	1.2	1.1
Niacin, mg	30.4	29.1	17.0	16.5(c)	17.8
Vitamin C, mg	0	0	15-30	0	0
Vitamin D, ug	0	0	0(d)	0	0

► (a) White corn supplies no vitamin A, where as yellow corn supplies 49 RE (Retinol equivalent, a measure of vitamin A value) per 100 grams dry weight. Most corn in the United States is yellow corn.

► (b) If a diet contains animal protein such as meat, eggs, or milk, the recommended protein would be less than 55g per day. If all raw protein is from milk or eggs, only 41g per day is required.

► (c) The niacin in corn is not fully available unless corn is treated with an alkali. Mexicans and Americans in the South and Southeast add lime or ashes to the water in which they soak or boil corn kernels.

► (d) Although adults do not need vitamin D, Infants and pregnant and lactating women should receive 10 ug. (10 micrograms).

18 - 9 Expedient Ways To Supply Deficient Essential Nutrients
(Simply keeping a good supply of multivitamin pills will eliminate a lot of hassle.)
Vitamin C

A deficiency of vitamin C (ascorbic acid) causes scurvy. This deadly scourge would be the first nutritional disease to afflict people having only grain and/or beans and lacking the know-how needed to sprout them and produce enough vitamin C. Within only 4 to 6 weeks of eating a ration containing no vitamin C, the first system of scurvy would appear: swollen and bleeding gums. This would be followed be weakness, then large bruises, hemorrhages, and wounds that would not heal. Finally, death from hemorrhages and heart failure would result.

One good expedient way to prevent or cure scurvy is to eat sprouted seeds -- not just the sprouts. Sprouted beans prevented scurvy during a famine in India. Captain James Cook was able to keep his sailors from developing scurvy during a three-year voyage by having them drink daily an unfermented beer made from dried, sprouted barley. For centuries the Chinese have prevented scurvy during the long winters or northern China by consuming sprouted beans.

Only 10 mg of vitamin C taken each day (1/5 of the smallest vitamin C tablet) is enough to prevent scurvy. If a little over an ounce (about 30 grams) of dry beans or dry wheat is sprouted until the sprouts are a little longer than the seeds, the sprouted seeds will supply 10 or 15 mg of vitamin C. Such sprouting, if done at normal room temperature, requires about 48 hours. To prevent sickness and to make sprouting beans more digestible, the sprouted seeds should be boiled in water for not longer than 2 minutes. Longer cooking will destroy too much vitamin C.

Usual sprouting methods produce longer sprouts than are necessary when production of enough vitamin C is the objective. These methods involve rinsing the sprouting seeds several times a day in safe water. First the seeds to be sprouted are picked clean of trash and broken seeds. Then the seeds are covered with water and soaked for about 12 hours. Next, the water is drained off and the soaked, swollen beans are placed on the inside of a plastic bag or a jar in a layer no more than an inch deep. If a plastic bag is used, you should make two loose rolls of paper, crumble them a little, dampen them, and place them inside the bag, along its sides. These two dampened paper rolls keep the plastic from resting on the seeds and form an air passage down the center of the bag. Wet paper should be placed in the mouth of the bag or jar so as to leave an air opening of only about 1 square inch. If this paper is kept moist, the seeds will remain sufficiently damp while receiving enough circulating air to prevent molding. They will sprout sufficiently after about 48 hours at normal temperature.

Sprouting seeds also increases their content of riboflavin, niacin, and folic acid. Sprouted beans are more digestible than raw, unsprouted beans, but not as easily digested or nourishing as are sprouted beans that have been boiled or sautéed for a couple of minutes. Sprouting is not a substitute for cooking. Contrary to the claims of some health food publications, sprouting does not increase the protein content of seeds, nor does it improve protein quality. Furthermore, sprouting reduces the caloric value of seeds. The warmth generated by germinating seeds reduces their energy value somewhat, as compared to unsprouted seeds.
Vitamin A

Well-nourished adults have enough vitamin A stored in their livers to prevent vitamin A deficiency problems for months, even if their diet during that time contains none of this essential vitamin. Children will be affected by deficiencies sooner than adults. The first symptom is an inability to see well in dim light. Continuing deficiency causes changes in body tissues. Lack of vitamin A in infants and children can result in stunted growth and serious eye problems -- even blindness. Therefore, a survival diet should be adequate in vitamin A as soon as possible, with children having priority.

Milk, butter, and margarine are common vitamin A sources that would not be available to most survivors if extensive Germ warfare including attacks on the power grid occurred. If these were no longer available yellow corn, carrots, and green, leafy vegetables (including dandelion greens) would be the best source. If these foods were not obtainable, the next best source would be sprouted whole-kernel wheat or other grains -- if seeds could be sprouted for three days in light so that the sprouts are green. Although better than no source, sprouting is not a very satisfactory way to meet vitamin A requirements. The development of fibrous roots makes 3-day sprouting wheat kernels difficult to eat, and, one must eat a large amount of seeds with green sprouts and roots to satisfy the recommended daily emergency requirements -- up to 5 1/2 cups of 5-day sprouted alfalfa seeds.

Vitamin D

Without vitamin D, calcium is not adequately absorbed. As a result, infants and children would develop rickets, a disease of defective bone mineralization. A massive Germ Warfare attack directed against our dairy cattle would cut off the vast majority of Americans from their main source of vitamin D, fortified milk.

Vitamin D can be formed in the body if the skin is exposed to the ultraviolet rays of the sun. Infants should be exposed to the sunlight very cautiously, initially for only a few minutes. In cold weather, maximum exposure of skin to sunlight is best done in a shallow pit shielded from the wind.

Niacin And Calcium

Niacin deficiency causes pellagra -- a disease that results in weakness, a rash on skin exposed to the sun, severe diarrhea, and mental deterioration. If a typical modern American had a diet primarily of corn and lacked the foods that normally supply niacin, symptoms of pellagra would first appear in about 6 months.

During the first part of this century, pellagra killed thousands of Americans in the South each year. These people had corn for their principal staple and ate few animal protein foods or beans. Yet Mexicans, who eat even more corn than did those Southerners, and even fewer foods of animal origin, did not suffer from pellagra.

The Mexican's freedom from pellagra is mainly due to their traditional method of soaking and boiling their dried corn in a lime-water solution. They use either dry, unslaked lime (calcium oxide, a dangerously corrosive substance made by roasting limestone) or dry slaked lime (calcium hydroxide, made by adding water to unslaked lime). Dry lime weighing about 1% as much as the dry corn is added to the soak water, producing an alkaline solution. Wood ashes also can be used instead of lime to make an alkali solution. The alkali treatment of corn makes the niacin available to the human body. Tables 18.1 and 18.2 show corn as having adequate niacin. However, the niacin in dried corn is not readily available to the body unless the corn has received an alkali treatment.

Treating corn with lime has another nutritional advantage: the low calcium content of corn is significantly increased.

Fat

The emergency recommendation for fat is slightly over 1 ounce per day (30 grams) of fat or cooking oil. This amount of fat provides only 10% of the calories in the emergency diet, which does not specify a greater amount because fats would be scarce after an extended

Biological attack. This amount is very low when compared to the average diet eaten in this country, in which fat provides about 40% of the calories. It would be difficult for many Americans to consume sufficient calories to maintain normal weight and morale without a higher fat intake; more fat should be made available as soon as possible. Increased fat intake is especially important for young children to provide calories needed for normal growth and development. Tests have shown that toddlers and old people, especially, prefer considerably more oil added to grain mush than the emergency recommendation of 10%.

Animal Protein

Vitamin B-12 is the only essential nutrient that is available in nature solely from animal sources. Since a normal person has a 2 to 4 year supply of vitamin B-12 stored in their liver, a deficiency should not develop before enough food of animal origin would again be available.

Many adults who are strict vegetarians keep in good health for years without any animal sources of food by using grains and beans together. It is more difficult to maintain normal growth and development in young children on vegetarian diets. When sufficient animal sources of food are available, enough should be provided to supply 7 grams of animal protein daily. This should be provided by about 1.4 ounces (38 grams) of lean meat, 0.7 ounces (20 grams) of nonfat dry milk, or one medium sized egg. When supplies are limited, young children should be given priority. Again: A little of these high-grade supplementary protein foods should be eaten with every meal.

18 - 10 A Basic Survival Ration To Store

A ration composed of the basic foods listed below in Table 18.3 provides about 2600 calories per day and is nutritionally balanced. It keeps better than a ration of typical American foods, requires much less space to store or transport, and is much less expensive. (A different emergency ration should be stored for infants and very small children, as will be explained in the following section.) Tests have indicated that the majority of Americans will find these basic foods acceptable under crisis conditions. In normal times, however, no one should store this or any other emergency food supply until they have prepared, eaten, and found its components satisfactory.

Unprocessed grains and beans provide adequate nourishment for many millions of the world's people who have little else to eat. Dry grains and beans are very compact: a 5 gallon can holds about 38 pounds of hard wheat. Yet when cooked, dry whole grains become bulky and give a well-fed feeling -- a distinct advantage if it is necessary to go on short rations during a prolonged crisis.

This basic ration has two disadvantages: (1) it requires cooking, and (2) Americans are unaccustomed to such a diet. Cooking can be minimized by having a grain grinding device. The disadvantage of starting to eat unaccustomed foods at a stressful time can be lessened by eating more whole grains and beans in normal times. Thereby, incidentally, saving money and improving the typical American's diet by reducing fat and increasing bulk and fiber.

When storing enough of this ration to last for several months or a year, it is best to select several kinds of beans for variety and nutrition. If soybeans are included, take into account the differences between soybeans and common beans as noted earlier in this chapter.

In many areas it is difficult to buy wheat and beans at prices nearly as low as the farmer receives for these commodities. However, in an increasing number of communities, at least one store sells whole-grain wheat and beans in large sacks at reasonable prices. Mormons, who store food for a range of possible personal and national disaster, are often the best source of information about where to get basic foods in quantity and at reasonable cost. (NITRO-PACK PREPAREDNESS CENTER 151 NORTH MAIN ST. HEBER CITY UTAH 84032 1-800-866-4876 is an excellent source fore these supplies.)

Soon after purchase, bulk foods should be removed from sacks (but not necessarily from sealed-plastic liner-bags) and sealed in metal containers or in thick-walled plastic containers for storage. Especially in the more humid parts of the United States, grain and beans should be frequently checked for moisture. If necessary, these foods should be dried out and rid of insects as described later in this chapter.

Vegetable oil stores as well in plastic bottles as in glass ones. The toughness and lightness of plastic bottles make them better than glass for carrying (forced evacuation) or using in a shelter. Since a pound of oil provides about 2 1/4 times as much energy as does a pound of sugar, dry grain, or milk powder, storing additional vegetable oil is an efficient way to improve a grain diet and make it more like the 40%-fat diet of typical Americans.

All multivitamin pills providing 5000 International Units (1500 mg retinol equivalent) vitamin A, 400 IU (10 mg) of vitamin D, and 50 to 100 mg of vitamin C, must meet U. S. Government standards, so the less expensive are usually quite adequate. Storage in a refrigerator generally lengthens the time before vitamin pills must be replaced with fresh ones. Because vitamin C is so essential, yet very inexpensive and long-lasting, it is prudent to store a large bottle.

It would be wise to have on hand ready-to-eat compact foods for use during a week or two in a home, along with those normally kept in the kitchen. (NITRO-PACK PREPAREDNESS CENTER 151 NORTH MAIN ST. HEBER CITY UTAH 84032 1-800-866-4876 is an excellent source fore these supplies.) All large food stores sell the following concentrated foods: non-fat milk powders, canned peanuts, compact ready-to-eat dry cereals such as Grape Nuts, canned meat and fish, white sugar, vegetable oil in plastic bottles, iodized salt, and daily multivitamin pills. If home occupants have a way to boil water (kerosene cookstove), it is advisable to include rice, noodles, and an "instant" cooked cereal such as oatmeal or wheat as well as coffee and tea for those who habitually drink these beverages.

Parched grain is a ready-to-eat food that has been used for thousands of years. Whole-kernel wheat, corn, and rice can be parched by the following method: Place the kernels about 1/4 inch deep in a pan, a skillet, or a tin can while shaking it over a flame, hot coals, or a red hot electric burner. The kernels will puff and brown slightly when parched. These parched grains are not difficult to chew and can be ground to a meal more easily than can raw kernels. Parched grain stores well if kept dry and free of insects.

TABLE 18.3
A BASIC SURVIVAL RATION FOR MULTI-YEAR STORAGE

A = Ounces Per Day.   C = Pounds For 30 Days Full Ration.

B = Grams Per Day.   D = Kilograms For 30 Days Full Ration.

	A	B	C	D
Whole-Kernel hard wheat	16	454	30.0	13.6
Beans	5	142	9.4	4.3
Non-fat milk powder	2	57	3.8	1.7
Vegetable oil	1	28	1.9	0.9
Sugar	2	57	3.8	1.7
Salt (iodized)	1/3	10	0/63	0.3
Total Weights	26 1/3	748	49.5	22.5
Multi-vitamin pills:		1 pill each day		

18 - 11 Emergency Food For Babies

Infants and very young children would be the first victims of starvation after a heavy terrorist Germ Warfare attack, especially if the electrical power grid was targeted, unless special preparations are made on their behalf. Unprocessed foods, which could prevent the majority of survivors from dying of hunger, would not be suitable for the very young. They need foods that are more concentrated and less rough. Most American mothers do not nurse their infants, and if the supply of baby foods was exhausted the parents might experience the agony of seeing their baby slowly starve.

To make a formula adequate for 24-hour period, the quantities of instant non-fat dry milk, vegetable cooking oil, and sugar listed in the "Per Day" column of Table 18.4 should be added to 4 cups of water. This formula can be prepared daily in cool weather or when a refrigerator is available. In warm or hot weather, or under unsanitary conditions, it is safer to make a formula 3 times a day. To do so, add 1/3 cup plus 2 teaspoons (a little less than an ounce) of instant non-fat milk powder to 1 1/3 cups (2/3 pints) of boiled water, and stir thoroughly. Then add 1 tablespoon (about 1/3 ounce, or 9 grams) of vegetable oil and 2 teaspoons of sugar, and stir. (If regular bakers' milk powder is used, 1/4 cup is enough when making one-third of the daily formula, 3 times a day.) If baby bottles are not at hand, milk can be spoon-fed to in infant.

Especially during a Germ war crisis, the best and most dependable food for an infant is mother's milk -- provided the mother is assured an adequate diet. The possibility of disaster is one more reason why a mother should nurse her baby for a full year. Storing additional high-protein foods and fats for a nursing mother usually will be better insurance against her infant getting sick or starving than keeping adequate stocks of baby foods and the equipment necessary for sanitary feeding after evacuation (with germ warfare, an evacuation could only spread the germs further afield) or an attack (with terrorism, there is little likelihood of any warning.)

To give a daily vitamin supplement to a baby, a multivitamin pill should be crushed to a fine powder between two spoons and dissolved in a small amount of fluid, so that the baby can easily swallow it. An infant that does not receive adequate amounts of vitamins A, D, and C will develop deficiency symptoms in 1 to 3 months, depending on the amounts stored in their body. Vitamin C deficiency, the first to appear, can be prevented by giving an infant 15 mg of vitamin C each day (about 1/3 of a 50-mg vitamin C tablet, pulverized) or customary foods containing vitamin C, such as orange juice. Lacking these sources, the juice squeezed from sprouting grains or legumes can be used. If no vitamin pills or foods rich in vitamin D are available, exposure of the baby's skin will cause their body to produce vitamin D. Initial exposure should be very short, no more than 10 minutes.

If sufficient milk is not obtainable even infants younger than six months should be given solid foods. Solid foods for babies must be pureed to a fine texture. Using a modern baby food grinder makes pureeing quick and easy work. Especially under germ warfare crisis conditions, a grinder should be cleaned and disinfected like other baby-feeding utensils, as described later in this section.

Several expedient methods are available: The food can be pressed through a sieve, mashed with a fork or spoon, or squeezed through a porous cloth. Good sanitation must be maintained; all foods should be brought to a boil after pureeing to insure that the food is safe from bacteria.

A pureed solid baby food can be made by first boiling together 3 parts of a cereal grain and 1 part of beans until they are soft. Then the mixture should be pressed through a sieve. The sieve catches the tough hulls from the grain kernels and the skins from the beans. The grain and beans combination will provide needed calories and a well-supplemented protein. The beans also supply the additional iron that a baby needs by the time they are 6 months old. Flowers made from whole grains or beans, as previously described, also can be used; however, these may contain rough material.

Some grains are preferable to others. It is easier to sieve cooked corn kernels than cooked wheat kernels. Since wheat is the grain most likely to cause allergies, it should not be fed to an infant until they are 6 to 7 months old if other grains, such as rice or corn, are available.

Small children also need more protein than can be supplied by grains alone. As a substitute for milk, some bean food should be provided at every meal. If the available diet is deficient in a concentrated energy source such as fat or sugar, a child's feeding should be increased to 4 or 5 times a day to enable them to assimilate more. Whenever possible, a small child should have a daily diet that contains at least one ounce of fat (3 tablespoons without scraping the spoon). This would provide more than 10% of a young child's calories in the form of fat, which would be beneficial.

If under emergency conditions it is not practical to boil infant's utensils, they can be sterilized with a bleach solution. Add one teaspoon of ordinary household bleach to each quart of water. (Ordinary household bleach contains 5.25% sodium hypochlorite as the only active ingredient and supplies approximately 5% available chlorine. If the strength to the bleach is unknown, add 3 teaspoons per quart). Directions for safe feeding without boiling are:

The Utensils (Include at least one 1-quart and one 1-pint mason jar for keeping prepared formula sterile until used).
1. Immediately after feeding, wash the inside and outside of all utensils used to prepare the formula and to feed the infant.
2. Fill a covered container with clean, cold water and add the appropriate amount of chlorine bleach.

3. Totally immerse all utensils until the next feeding (3 or 4 hours). Be sure that the bottle, if used, is filled with bleach solution. Keep it covered.
AT FEEDING TIME
1. Wash hands before preparing food.
2. Remove utensils from the disinfectant chlorine solution and drain. Do not rinse or dry.
3. Prepare formula; feed the baby.
4. Immediately after feeding, wash utensils in clean water and immerse again in the disinfectant solution.
5. Prepare fresh chlorine solution each day.

TABLE 18.4   EMERGENCY FOOD SUPPLY FOR ONE BABY

INGREDIENTS	PER DAY VOLUME AND OUNCES	GRAMS	PER MONTH POUNDS	KILOGRAMS	PER 6 MONTHS POUNDS	KILOGRAMS
Instant non-fat dry milk	1 cup plus 2 tablespoons (2 1/4 oz.)	8	6	2.72	32	15
Vegetable cooking oil	3 tablespoons (1 oz.)	30	2	0.90	12	5.5
Sugar	2 tablespoons (0.7 oz.)	20	1.3	0.60	8	3.6
Standard daily multi-vitamin pills	1/3 pill		10 pills		60 Pills	

18.12 Storage Of Foods

Whole grains and white sugar can be stored successfully for decades. Dried beans, non-fat milk powder, and vegetable oil can be stored for several years. Some rules for good storage are:

Keep Food Dry

The most dependable way to ensure continuing dryness is to store dry grain in metal containers, such as ordinary 5-gallon metal storage cans or 55 gallon metal drums with gasket lids. Full 5-gallon cans are light enough to be easily carried in an automobile.

Particularly in humid areas, grain that seems to be dry often is not dry enough to store for a long period. To be sure that the grain is dry enough to store for years use a drying agent. The best drying agent for this purpose is silica gel with color indicator. The gel is blue when it is capable of absorbing water, pink when it needs to be heated to become an effective drying agent again. Silica gel is inexpensive if bought from chemical supply firms located in most cities. By heating it in a hot oven or in a pan over a fire until it turns blue again, silica gel can be used repeatedly for years.

The best containers for the silica gel used to dry grain (or to determine its dryness) are homemade cloth envelopes large enough for a heaping cupful of the gel. A clear plastic window should be stitched in, through which color changes can be observed. Put an envelope of silica gel on top of the grain in a 5-gallon can filled to within a couple of inches of its top. Then close the can tightly. Even a rather loose-fitting lid can be sealed tightly with tape. If after a few days the silica gel is still blue, the grain is dry enough. If the silica gel has turned pink, repeat the process with fresh envelopes until it can be seen that the grain is dry.

Keep Grains And Beans Free Of Weevils, Other Insects, And Rodents.

Dry ice (carbon dioxide) is the safest means still widely available to the public for ridding grain and beans of insects. Place about 4 ounces of dry ice on top of the grain in a five gallon metal container. Put the lid on somewhat loosely so that air in the grain can be driven out of the can. (This will happen as the dry ice vaporizes and the heavy carbon dioxide sinks into the grain and displaces the air around the kernels.) After an hour or two, tighten the lid and seal it with tape. After one month, all insects in this carbondioxide atmosphere will have died from lack of oxygen.

Store Foods In The Coolest Available Place, Out Of The Light.

Remember that the storage life of most foods is cut in half by an increase of 18 degrees F (10 C) in storage temperature. 48 months of storage at 52 F is equivalent to 24 months at 70 F, and to 12 months at 88 F.

Do Not Place Stored Metal Containers Directly On The Floor

To avoid possible condensation of moisture and rusting that result, place containers on spaced boards. For long-term storage in damp basements, use solid-plastic containers with thick walls.

Rotate Stored Foods

Eat the oldest food of each type and replace it with fresh food. Although cooking oil and non-fat milk powder remain edible after several years of storage at room temperature, these and most other dry foods are more nourishing and taste better if stored for no more than 2 years. Most canned foods taste better if kept no more than one year. Exceptions are whole grains and white sugar, which stay good for decades if stored properly.

Chapter 19
Colloidal Silver
(Your Personal Portable Pharmacy)

Silver is a powerful, natural shield and antibiotic that has been used for thousands of years. Ancient Greeks lined their eating and drinking vessels with silver, as did many other cultures throughout the world. Pioneers of the American West would put a silver dollar in a jug of milk to keep it fresh without refrigeration. Did you ever wonder why silverware was made from silver? One of the properties of silver is that it kills bacteria on contact in six minutes or less. It may be that gold and silver were first used as valued currency because of their medical properties. In Biblical times, herdsmen would often "bury" ingots in their wells and fiercely defend this "sweet water".

Colloidal Silver is the result of an electromagnetic process that pulls microscopic particles from a larger piece of silver into a liquid, such as water. These microscopic particles can be more easily absorbed and travel through the body. Colloidal Silver works as a catalyst, disabling the enzyme that all one celled bacteria, fungi and viruses use for their oxygen metabolism. In short, the bad guys suffocate. Unlike our experience with antibiotics, resistant strains have never been known to develop the ability to withstand the effects of silver. In fact, antibiotics are only effective against perhaps a dozen forms of bacteria and fungi, but never against viruses. Because no known disease-causing organism can live in the presence of even minute traces of the chemical element of metallic silver, Colloidal Silver is effective against more than 650 different disease causing pathogens including viruses.

The body doesn't develop a tolerance to silver. Colloidal silver is both a remedy and a prevention of infections of any kind. Sufficient colloidal silver in your body is equivalent to a second immune system.Unlike silver in its compound forms (for example silver nitrate), silver in the colloidal state, may be applied in a much more concentrated form, with correspondingly better results. All fungus, virus, bacterium, streptococcus, staphylococcus, and other pathogenic organisms are killed in three or four minutes; in fact, there is no microbe known that is not killed by colloidal silver in six minutes or less, in a dilution of as little as five parts per million.There are also no side effects whatsoever from higher concentrations.

Colloidal silver contains no free radicals, as the silver acts only as a catalyst, and is stabilized. Colloidal silver is not a chemical compound containing silver, but pure metallic silver of submicroscopic clusters of just a few atoms, held in suspension in pure water, by the tiny electric charge on each atom. It is absolutely non-toxic (except to one celled plants and animals), and non-addicting.

It would appear highly unlikely that even germ warfare agents could survive an encounter with Colloidal Silver, since viruses like E Bola and Hanta, or even the dreaded "flesh-eating bacteria" are, in the end, merely hapless viruses and bacteria. To top it off, Colloidal Silver is virtually non-toxic, making it safe for both children and adults, as well as pets. In short, anything bigger than a one cell animal seems to like it.

Nor does one have to worry about that FDA (Food and Drug Administration) fox being put in charge of this home remedy hen house. Colloidal Silver is a pre-1938 healing modality, making it exempt from FDA jurisdiction under the grandfather clause.

BACTERIOLOGICAL WARFARE

It is true that consuming large amounts over long periods of time may kill some friendly bacteria in your intestines. If taking large amounts, you should supplement your diet with yogurt or acidophilus, or compensate for possible bacteria loss in some other way. This is not, however, a serious problem, and unlike antibiotics, Colloidal Silver does not weaken the body's immune system. In fact, it is said to give the body a second immune system, creating a shield against disease of all kinds.

ESTABLISHED USAGE

Take approximately 1 oz. (of 5-15 ppm) morning and night for a maintenance dose and take 8-10 oz. or more if we feel a cold or sore throat coming on.
It's also a good idea to shake the container that you keep the colloid in before use as there may be a little settling. Commercial colloid is made with electrically charged water to help keep the silver in a colloid state for a longer period of time, but even it will settle over a period of months. Properly prepared and properly stored collodial silver may last up to a year.

Colloidal silver can be applied directly to cuts, scrapes and open sores; or put a few drops on a small Band-Aid and wear over warts, cuts, abrasions, or any open sore; or dab directly onto eczema or such itchy areas, or acne, mosquito bites, or any skin problem.

Water is purified by adding one half-teaspoon per gallon, shake well, wait six minutes and drink. Mixed in this way it's tasteless. Occasionally drink two quarts of this purified water over a day's time, especially with meals as a great digestive aid, because it eliminates fermentation.

It is the ideal food preservative, because it is also good for you. Use in canning at one-quarter teaspoon per quart, for example:

Those already using colloidal silver report that they catch milder, fewer if any, colds or flu. The emphasis is on the prevention of all infections. There are no known side effects. There is no known harm to the liver, kidneys, any other organ, system or any part of the body in its colloidal form. No one has ever overdosed, regardless of the amount, as it is not at all an allopathic poison.

Parasites are also killed, as they have an egg stage in their reproductive cycle, which is one celled and therefore killed in six minutes or less. Human single cells are not effected because all of our cells gain their energy as a "mammalian mitochondria" system instead of the microbes' "cell membrane substrate" manner.

The adult RDA for silver is 400 milligrams. We suggest 10ppm per day as a maintenance dosage and 4 to 5 times that much in times of sickness or exposure to pathogens.
A good quality Colloidal Silver can be diluted as much as 8 to 1 and still be highly effective as long as the ppm (parts per million) does not drop below 5ppm. For instance colloidal silver containing 20ppm could be divided equally into 4 equal portions. However, there would appear to be a great deal of leeway here, since no toxic dose is known.

A FEW UNIQUE PLUS TRADITIONAL USES FOR SILVER COLLOID

When you control a source of high concentration silver colloid you can use it for hundreds of health improvement applications. A few are suggested here. You can use most tap water to make colloid for industrial and external uses and distilled or de-ionized water for internal or injectable applications.

Add to suspected drinking water when traveling or camping. Colloid sprayed burns heal rapidly without scarring. Safely sterilize anything from toothbrushes to surgical instruments. Use topically on cuts, wounds, abrasions, rashes, sunburn, razor nicks, bandages. Spray on garbage to prevent decay odors. Mist kitchen sponges, towels, cutting boards to eliminate E. Coli 0157:H7 and salmonella bacteria to prevent food poisoning, gastrointestinal inflammation, and genital tract infections.

Add when canning, preserving, bottling. Use like peroxide on zits and acne. Add to juices. Milk will delay spoiling fermenting, deteriorating, clabbering or curdling. Spray in shoes, between toes, between legs to stop most skin itch, athletes foot, fungi, jock itch. Diminish dandruff, psoriasis, skin rashes, etc. Add to bath water, gargle, douches, colon irrigation, nasal spray and dental water-pic solutions. Cuts downtime dramatically with colds, flu, pneumonia, staph, strep, respiratory infections and rhino viruses. Skin itch, eye and ear infections, some moles and warts vanish when colloid is sprayed on body after bathing. Use with Q-tip on fingernail, toenail, and ear fungi. Neutralize tooth decay and bad breath. Colloid stops halitosis by eliminating bacteria deep in throat and on back of tongue. Unlike pharmaceutical antibiotics, silver colloid never permits strain-resistant pathogens to evolve.

Put a few drops on band-aids and bandages to shorten healing times. Health professionals might consider IV and IM injections. Tumor and polyp shrinking is reported when masses are injected directed (when colloid is added to sterile physiological saline or Ringers Solutions which contains -9000 ppm sodium chloride). Toothaches, mouth sores, bacterial irritations are diminished. Soak dentures. Spray refrigerator, freezer and food storage bin interiors. Stop mildew and wood rot. Mix in postage stamp, envelope, and tape moistening wells, paint and paste pots to prevent bacterial growth, odors, spoiling or souring. Add to water based paints, wallpaper paste, dishwater, cleaning and mopping solutions etc. Spray pet bedding and let dry.

Spray on top of contents of opened jam, jelly and condiment containers and inside lids before replacing. Mix a little in pet water, birdbaths, cut flower vases. Always add to swamp cooler water. Spray air conditioner filters after cleaning. Swab air ducts and vents to prevent breeding sites for germs. Use routinely in laundry final rinse water and always before packing away seasonal clothes. Damp clothes or towels and washcloths will not sour or mildew. Eliminates unwanted microorganisms in planter soils and hydroponics systems. Spray plant foliage to stop fungi, molds, rot, and most plant diseases.

Treat pools, fountains, humidifiers, Jacuzzis, hot tubs, baths, dishwashers, recirculating cooling tower water, gymnasium foot dips, and bath and shower mats. Spray inside shoes, watch bands and gloves and under fingernails periodically. Treat shower stalls, tubs, fonts, animal watering troughs, shavers to avoid trading germs. Rinse fruit and vegetables before storing or using. Put in cooking water.

Human and animal shampoos become disinfectants. Prevent carpets, drapes, wallpaper from mildewing. Wipe telephone mouthpieces, pipe stems, headphones, hearing aids, eyeglass frames, hairbrushes, combs, loofas. Excellent for diapers and diaper rash. Wipe down toilet seats, bowls, tile floors, sinks, urinals, doorknobs. Kill persistent odors. Rinse invalid's pillowcases, sheets, towels and bedclothes.

There are literally thousand of other essential uses for this ridiculously inexpensive, odorless, tasteless, colorless, totally benign and easily produced powerful non-toxic disinfectant and healing agent. You'll find that a spray or misting bottle of silver colloid solution may be the most useful health enhancement tool in your environment.

GENERATE YOUR OWN COLLOIDAL SILVER

Making your own colloidal silver is very simple if you pay attention to several details. Everything except the .999 pure silver can be found at Radio Shack or other electronics parts stores.

Making Your Own Silver-Colloid Generator - What You Will Need

* Three 9-volt transistor radio batteries
* Three transistor battery snap-on lead connectors
* One "grain-of-wheat" light bulb, 24 to 28 volt, 40-mA
* 1 foot of two-conductor stranded insulated wire
* 10 " of .999 pure silver wire, (14 gauge is best). Cut in two-5 inch lengths.
* 1 foot heat-shrink tubing 1/8 inch (careful use of electrical tape is possible)
* 1 small plastic electronic project box   (to hold 3 batteries plus 1/2" longer)
* 1 female 1/8" jack (chassis mount)
* 1 male 1/8" plug
* 2 insulated alligator clips
* Soldering iron

Constructing the generator

1. Solder the battery snap-on lead connectors together in series (figure 1), red to black, leaving one red and one black wire free to solder to other components. Be sure, before soldering any two wires together, to cut a small piece of heat shrink tubing and slide over the wire and shrink the tubing over the soldered joint. The tubing can be shrunk by applying heat with a hair dryer, heat gun or judicious use of a cigarette lighter.
2. Take the free black wire from the battery snap-on connectors you just put together and solder it to one leg of the "grain-of-wheat" bulb. (figure 2)
3. Take the other leg of the "grain-of-wheat" bulb and solder it to one side of a 1/8" female jack. Then take the remaining red lead from the battery connectors and solder it to the other side of the 1/8" female jack. (Make sure that these are on electrically opposite legs, its easy to solder them to electrically common legs)
4. Drill two holes in one end of the project box, one to fit the chassis mount female 1/8" jack through and the other to fit the "grain-of-wheat" bulb through. The chassis mount jack fastens itself to the project box with a nut, however you may need to glue the

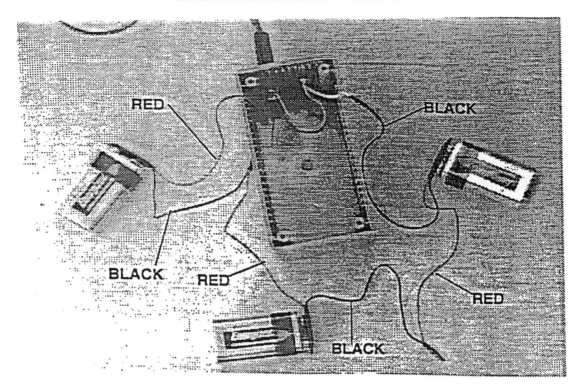

FIGURE 1

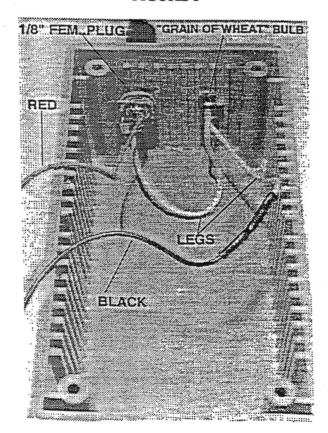

FIGURE 2

119

"grain-of-wheat" bulb into place. (the bulb may heat up and expand under use and crack , I'd glue it into a hole larger than itself)

5. The electrodes are constructed by soldering one end of the two-conductor stranded wire to the 1/8" male plug. Be careful when soldering each conductor of the wire to the plug not to short the circuit. To the other end solder the insulated alligator clips, the red clip to the red lead and the black to the black lead. You really don't need to be too concerned about the colors on the electrodes as long as the circuit is complete the generator will work.

6. Snap on three transistor batteries, carefully place them and the tucked wire into the box and put the lid on it. To see if everything is wired correctly, touch the alligator clips together. If the "grain-of-wheat" bulb lights up, the generator should be correctly wired. If the bulb doesn't light or stays on continually, compare your wiring with the accompanying diagrams. Closely inspect all your soldered joints, especially the solders at the 1/8" female jack and 1/8" male plug making sure the posts aren't touching each other causing a short circuit. If you have a voltage meter you can check the voltage between the two clips, it should be about 27 volts. The optimum voltage for colloidal silver production is about 30 volts, but 27 volts works just fine. If you don't have a voltage meter, don't worry, just touch the clips together again, if the bulb shines brightly every thing should be wired correctly. If the bulb is dimly lit, check the wiring of your batteries, the wires should be joined red to black (see photo).

Now you've built the generator itself, its time to produce the actual product...

INSTRUCTIONS FOR COLLOIDAL SILVER PRODUCTION

1. Pour distilled water into a glass (not metal) cup. Because your wire is extra long, it will accommodate a 16-ounce tumbler.

2. Add one drop or less of saline solution for every 4 ounces of water. Saline solution must be made from sea salt.* Spring water--for topical applications--may already have enough saline to promote conductivity without adding saline solution.

3. Stir contents with plastic (non-conductive) utensil.

4. Insert your two .999 fine silver wires**(see caution below) into water so that the ends fold over the top rim of glass. Do not let wires touch each other or the process will stop.

5. Plug the alligator clips into generator. Briefly touch alligator clips together and watch how brightly the generator bulb flashes. This is a good way to check the strength of the batteries. Next, take one alligator clip and attach it to one of the silver wire ends that extend over rim and outside of cup. Attach second alligator clip to the end of the second silver wire extending over rim. You cannot shock yourself in this process.

6. Process will begin. Do not be concerned if bulb glows very dimly.

7. Observe bubbles of hydrogen rise from one silver wire, while an ultra fine, silver mist begins to peel off the other. For each minute of activation in a 16 ounce glass and using properly conductive water, a silver colloid of approximately 1 part per million (ppm) will be created. Five minutes should produce a high quality working solution. Yield depends on water volume (size of glass), water conductivity, surface area of electrodes, amount of current, and time. Within limits, higher concentrations of silver colloid can be generated by increasing the time.

8. To finish, detach alligator clips. Process will stop. Dry silver wires with paper towel. To remove the dark oxide on the silver electrode wire, polish the blackened wire with small

nylon kitchen scouring pad. Unplug the clips for storage. This will prevent accidental discharge of your batteries.

STORAGE

Rinse out hydrogen peroxide bottles, or any other dark-non conductive container, to store colloidal silver. Keep in cool, dark place. Do not refrigerate. Always shake bottle before using to evenly distribute silver colloid. Do not store near speaker cabinets or other strong magnetic fields. Full potency can be retained for at least a month, maybe two, when properly stored.

*MAKING SALINE SOLUTION

Pour four ounces of distilled water into a separate glass container. Add one level teaspoon of sea salt and stir. Do not use common table salt, as it has chemical additives. After stirring the salt solution, pour some of the water into an eyedropper bottle.

** SILVER ELECTRODES CAUTION

Do NOT use sterling silver as it contains nickel which could be TOXIC.Possibly the best source for .999 pure silver is your custom jeweler. Make sure your jeweler knows that his source is reputable and that the silver he is purchasing for you is truly .999 fine silver.

BACTERIOLOGICAL WARFARE

TESTIMONIALS

1) Dr. Robert O Becker, "The Body Electric "(William Morrow & Co. 1985), recognized a correlation between low silver levels and sickness. He said silver deficiency was responsible for the improper functioning of the immune system. Dr. Becker's experiments conclude that silver works on the full spectrum of pathogens without any side effects or damage to the body. He also states that silver does more than without any side effects or damage to the body. He also states that silver was doing something more than killing disease causing organisms. It was also causeing major growth stimulation of injured tissues. Burn patients and even elderly patients notice more rapid healing. And he discovered that all cancer cells can change back to normal cells. All strains of pathogens resistant to other antibiotics are killed by silver.

2) "Use of Colloids in Health and Disease." Colloidal Silver is proven particularly effective in cases of intestinal troubles. Dr. Henry Crooks found that Silver in the colloidal state is highly germicidal, quite harmless to humans and absolutely non-toxic. Rather than in a chemical compound, the Silver, in the colloidal state, may be applied in a much more concentrated form, with correspondingly better results. All fungus, virus, bacterium, streptococcus, staphylococcus, and other pathogenic organisms are killed in three or four minutes; in fact, there is no microbe known that is not killed Colloidal Silver in six minutes or less, a dilution of as little as five parts per million, though there are no side effects whatsoever from high concentrations. Provo Herald, Feb 2, 1992, pg D1: Colloidal Silver as a cure AIDS.

3) "(Colloidal Silver) is not a chemical compound containing Silver, but pure metallic silver of submicroscopic clusters of just a few atoms, held in suspension in pure water, by the tiny electric charge on each atom." Health Consciousness, Vol. 15, No. 4.

4) As an antibiotic, silver kills over 650 disease causing organisms; resistant strains fail to develop. Silver is absolutely non-toxic. Silver is the best all-around germ fighter we have. Doctors are reporting that, taken internally, it works against syphilis, cholera, and malaria, diabetes and severe burns. Bio/Tech News, 1995

5) Dr. Bjorn Nordstrom, of the Karolinska Institute, Sweden, has used Silver in his cancer cure method for many years. He says the whole thing is quite simple. This brought rapid remission in patients given up by other doctors. "Silver, Our Mightiest Germ Fighter: Science Digest, March 10/78

6) Metallic Silver (Colloid) is not toxic, however, silver nitrate and other compounds of silver are and should not be ingested. Dr. Bob Beck

7) Environmental Protection Agency's Poison Control Center reports no toxicity listing for Colloidal Silver, considering it harmless in any concentration.

8) The FDA has stated that because Colloidal Silver is (by fifty; ;years) a pre-1938 drug, it may continue to be marketed. Sept 13, 1991, letter received from consumer safety officer Harold

Davis, U.S., Food and Drug Administration. Moreover, the FDA has no jurisdiction regarding a pure, mineral element.

9) American Drug Index, section on Inorganic Pharmaceutical Chemistry, recognized silver for its germicidal action, calling a stabilized form, "Mild Silver Protein". There are several forms of Mild Silver Protein.

10) "Silver, Our Mightiest Germ Fighter", March 1978. As an antibiotic, silver kills over 650 disease causing organisms; resistant strains fail to develop. Silver is absolutely non-toxic. Silver is the best all-around germ fighter we have. Doctors are reporting that, taken internally, it works against syphilis, cholera, and malaria, diabetes and severe burns. Richard L. Davies, executive director of the Silver Institute, which monitors silver technology in 37 countries, reports, "In four years we've described 67 important new medical uses for silver".

DISCLAIMER: This article on Colloidal Silver has been written and presented strictly for information and educational purposes only. We are not prescribing treatment for any person or condition. The information contained in these instructions should be used for experimental and research purposes only. Pregnant and lactating women should consult with their physician before applying any information contained in these instructions. Persons who have had organ transplants should also consult with their physician as colloidal silver has been shown to boost the body's own immune response, therefore use of colloidal silver would be contraindicated.
The information conveyed herein is based on pharmacological and other records both ancient and modern. We make no claims whatsoever as to any specific benefits accruing from the use of colloidal silver. Testimonials from enthusiastic users are for your information only and are not meant to imply that you will experience similar benefits or results. The value of and the benefits and results derived from the use of colloidal silver are subjective due to variable individual health factors and metabolic differences which tend to make the formula more or less adaptogenic.

HOW TO GET READY

In the event of outbreaks of biological plagues, those who have already been taking sufficient levels of colloidal silver will have an automatic resistance in their bodies. They may also take any antibiotics without fear of interaction problems.

If, however, a person has not been taking colloidal silver for 30 to 50 days prior to exposure to a plague, silver will have little effect. This is because invading bacteria can kill within several days, while it takes weeks for colloidal silver to be spread through your entire body's millions of cells.

While a daily dosage is approximately 1 oz/day (of colloidal silver in the 5 to 15 ppm range), during an attack the dosage should be at least 4 oz/ day. In fact, if enough colloidal silver is available, it is recommended that all liquids taken into the body should have silver in them. This step will purify many food sources from possible contamination. Remember that colloidal silver will only work for you if it is in your system before you are exposed to pathogens.

We know that some of you will not be able to construct your own generator. For that reason, we are grateful that Millennial Technologies has agreed to provide colloidal silver to our readers at approximately 1/4 the current market price. This product is made from certified pure distilled water, pure .999 silver and the final product is assay certified as to its ppm level by an outside laboratory. They also carry small, family size colloidal silver generators and .999 pure silver electrodes to enable you to supply your own needs. We feel that prudent people should begin this low cost protection now.

You may reach Millennial Technologies at 1-888-833-0515 or fax at 1-405-478-4352 for prices and ordering information.

SOME PERSONAL THOUGHTS

I know that this book contains some frightening information. The purpose in presenting it to you is not to cause you to panic, but rather cause you to take appropriate action.

It is important to remember that God has a plan. He is moving in the course of human affairs to reclaim planet earth and all of mankind who will accept his plan of salvation (being saved from destruction). After all, God is the Creator and thereby the rightful owner of all of creation. So with the knowledge of what may shortly come to pass in America , how do you make things right with God?

1. First acknowledge God as the rightful owner.
   Collossians 1:16,17   For by Him were all things created, that are in Heaven, and that are in earth, visible and invisible, whether they be thrones, or dominions, or principalities, or powers: all things were created by Him and for Him: And He is before all things, and by Him all things consist.

2. Your rebellion (insisting on doing things your own way) is sin to God.
   Romans 3:23   For all have sinned and come short of the Glory of God.

3. Repent of your sins. (Decide to live differently according to God's plan)
   1 John 1:8   If we confess our sins, He is faithful and just to forgive us our sins and to cleanse us from all unrighteousness.

4. Acknowledge Jesus as your Lord (One who gives direction to your life)
   Romans 10:13   Whosoever shall call upon the name of the Lord shall be saved.

5. Live your life to please God.
   II Cor 5:9   We labor that we may be accepted by Him.

6. Read your Bible to find the rules for living
   Psalm 119:105   Thy Word is a lamp unto my feet and a light unto my path.

7. Remember God is able to keep you safe from anything.
   Psalm 91:7   A thousand shall fall at thy side and ten thousand at thy right hand; but it shall not come nigh thee.

God has always warned mankind when problems were ahead. Those who have listened to God and made preparations, history has called wise We pray that this information has been presented in such a way that you can hear God's warning and make decisions about what is to come.

SUMMARY

In the beginning of this book, I explained how I became acquainted with Mariam Arif from Iraq, who explained to me that North America would be subject to terrorist attacks using Germ Warfare. Of this I have no doubt. The following would be one of many possible scenarios.

A lady coming from the Middle East carries a single Plague vile in her body cavity and arrives in New York. Once she gets to her apartment, she retrieves the vile from her body cavity goes to the refrigerator, and takes out some skimmed milk. From the carton, she removes about 2 ml and places this in a small test tube. To this she adds another 2 ml of distilled water. She then breaks off the top of the Plague vial and adds the half- strength skimmed milk until the pellet at the bottom of the vial is thoroughly covered. She then sets this aside and takes out a 150 ml flask and to this she adds 100 ml distilled water and the appropriate amount of dehydrated medium (Nutrient broth will work). This is placed onto a very small and inexpensive heated shaker table. To this she now adds from the vial the now rehydrated plague, and lets it incubate for 10 days. All the while she has been taking Terramycin to keep her from becoming infected.

After ten days, she takes ten 12 ml screw top test tubes and removes from the 150 ml flask, 10 ml of the now very infectious plague and places 10 ml into each test tube. These are first refrigerated and brought down to 3 degrees centigrade. Earlier that day she has called ten accomplices, each of whom has taken a 4 gallon stainless steel spray container, to which they have added 3 gallons of water and 60 grams of Nutrient Broth dehydrated powder. The water in each was brought to a boil for about an hour and then removed from the heat and permitted to cool. Later that day the lady stops by and delivers to each accomplice one 10 ml Plague culture. This is added to the now cooled nutrient broth inside the stainless steel sprayer and a heating pad is wrapped around the outside to keep it about body temperature. An aquarium air stone has been placed into the tank and hooked up to a small air pump. This will remain for ten days. All during this time each accomplice is taking terramycin to keep from becoming infected.

After the ten days has elapsed, the lady and her ten accomplices meet one last time on the North American shore. The next time they meet they will be safely back in their own country. Each accomplice returns to his apartment and reinstalls the air pump back into the stainless steel sprayer, dons some appropriate looking clothing on which appears the word EXTERMINATOR, and sets out for his target. Five of the operatives head for the subway system and the other five target the air intake systems of the largest buildings in the financial district. With all the activities going on who is going to pay any attention to a maintenance person spraying for bugs? After they have delivered their deadly cargoes, they head for the airport and in a few hours are safely back inside their own countries. Nothing seems to be amiss until the morning of the third day when actually hundreds of thousands of people start to have severe respiratory problems and start coughing up blood. And with each cough they spray the air with deadly droplets of Plague. Anyone breathing this in only adds new cases to the already overwhelmed medical facilities. By the end of the third day the morgues are completely overwhelmed. By the beginning of the fourth day, 400,000 plus are dead, with no end in sight.

The Basic Facts

If a Germ Warfare terrorist attack broke out today, millions of Americans would die unnecessarily. Our country has never faced such a critical problem. A solution is possible, and can be set in motion, if we face three questions that must be answered. (1) Why has it happened ? (2) What can we do at this late date ? (3) What can individuals do?

1. WHY HAS IT HAPPENED ? There are three reasons:

Poor Priorities: This is not pleasant for Americans to face, but it is unavoidable. Our political leadership has not provided a program that will protect American lives, the most important asset in this country. The seeds for this oversight were planted in the 1950's when politics and budgets took precedence over the protection of American lives. The obligation upon leaders is that they lead. **Proper leadership requires telling the people the truth and meeting the high priority needs of the country.** The facts regarding Germ Warfare were known in the 1950's and are obvious today. Leadership fails when these facts are kept from public view and other more politically expedient courses followed. We must immediately get our priorities in order.

Poor Judgment:

During the 1970's our leaders were preoccupied with disarmament negotiations. During 1972-1973 our leaders signed the Anti-Biological warfare agreement to ban all forms of biological warfare, both offensive and defensive. To this they also attached the biological warfare civil defense program and the older concept of MAD (Mutual Assured Destruction). From this point our country has been totally vulnerable to biological weapons.

Each administration in the 1970's ignored the truth about Biological civil defense and ignored those who recommended telling the facts to the American people. Seemingly, each administration tried to grab the "brass ring" of disarmament. It was hoped that if arms limitations took place, then Biological Civil Defense would not be needed. Washington officials have been unable to see that an effective Biological civil defense program is necessary with or without disarmament. Who can predict the future? Does history teach us to be ever-vigilant? Who can rationalize the intentional exposure of millions of Americans to unnecessary Biological termination? The time has come to replace wishful thinking with common sense.

2. What Can Be Done At This Late Date?

There is only one answer. We must tell the truth to the American people. Recent surveys indicate 77% of Americans believe the country is on the "wrong track." Almost as many, 64%, believe the country is in "deep and serious trouble." In addition, a majority of Americans harbor a distrust for politicians. Are these views justified? Would Americans still feel this distrust was justified if they were told the truth? Could the fundamental reason for public distrust of politicians be that Americans know, subconsciously, that some basic breach of confidence has separated them from their elected representatives? If government cannot be trusted to provide survival .... what can it be trusted for?

If each Congressman, Governor and Mayor told the public where we stood regarding Biological civil defense, the changes would not be long delayed. A wave of support would launch the long overdue program. Only the truth can solve this central problem facing America today.

3. What Can You Do Now?

First, learn everything you can about the present situation. Get the facts; they will upset you but it's better to know the truth. Contact your State Health department and ask for available materials. **Devise a family survival plan on the assumption that no one will be able to help you but you yourself**. Prepare your family for whatever might come . If your ancestors had not done this, you wouldn't be here. Make some sacrifices, examine your priorities and meet the future with confidence and resolve. Americans may be gullible but they are not quitters. Second, work within the system for positive change. Everyone should write to his elected officials stating his or her beliefs. Then write again, and again. Confront your school board, the editor of your local paper, your church, your fellow workers and your neighbors with the facts. One person's voice can be clearly heard in Washington if the facts are correct. Third, pray for peace. Pray for your country and its leaders. Pray for the enemies of your country as well. Pray for wisdom so that you can help solve this national problem instead of being a part of it.

It is untrue that the public does not know what it wants; it wants Biological Civil Defense. Neither is it true that the public is apathetic. The public seems apathetic because it assumes that normal, prudent precautions have already been taken. The public does not know that the government has failed to provide the Biological civil defense program which will preserve our society in the event of Terrorist Germ Warfare attacks.

ACKNOWLEDGMENTS

* Department Of The Army And The Air Force Technical Manual N0. 3-216 Air Force Manual No. 355-6 Military Biology and Biological Warfare Agents.

* Headquarters Department Of The Army Field Manual No. 21-41 SOLDIERS HANDBOOK FOR CHEMICAL AND BIOLOGICAL OPERATIONS.

* Headquarters Department Of The Army Field Manual No. 8-230 MEDICAL SPECIALIST

* Kay B. Franz, Ph.D., Nutritionist, Assistant Professor, Food Science and Nutrition Department, Brigham Young University -- for information and advice used extensively in the food chapter.

BACTERIOLOGICAL WARFARE

NOTES